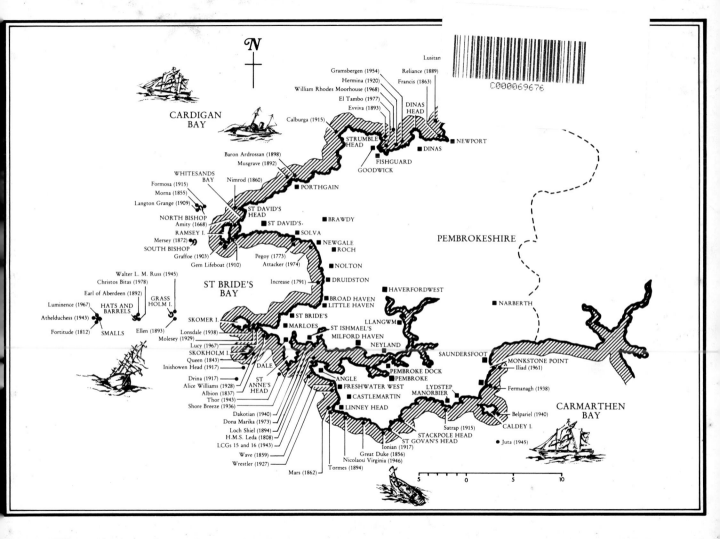

PEMBROKESHIRE SHIPWRECKS

TED GODDARD

CHRISTOPHER DAVIES

Copyright © 1983 Ted Goddard

First Published by
Hughes & Son (Publishers) Ltd.

Reprinted 1988 by
Christopher Davies (Publishers) Ltd.,
P.O. Box 403, Sketty,
Swansea, SA2 9BE.

ISBN 0 7154 0706 6

*Printed in Wales by
Dynevor Printing Company,
Rawlings Road, Llandybïe, Dyfed.*

Front Cover Illustration

The ill-fated cattle freighter EL TAMBO, her bows awash, sinks in Fishguard Harbour in March 1977.

(Picture: RAF Brawdy)

Back Cover Illustration

Three tugs, on passage from Liverpool to Piraeus in Greece, were wrecked near Solva in October 1981. One of the tugs is seen stranded on rocks, while the stern of another is just showing above the boiling seas. The tugs VERNICOS ALEXIA and VERNICOS BARBERA were being towed, in tandem, by a third, the VERNICOS GIORGOS. Off the Pembrokeshire coast, the VERNICOS GIORGOS fouled her propeller with the tow line and anchored in St. Brides Bay to free it. She dragged her anchors in a storm, however, and all three tugs were driven aground on The Cradle, Solva.

(Picture: Western Telegraph)

Acknowledgements

This book is not intended to be a definitive work on Pembrokeshire shipwrecks. So many ships have been lost on this beautiful, but deadly, coastline, that to attempt to refer to them all would be impossible. What I've aimed to do is to concentrate on some of the wrecks from the past 300 years or so and I am indebted to everyone who has given me help on my 'voyage' in major and minor ways.

I would particularly thank the hon. secretaries and coxswains of Pembrokeshire lifeboats, the Royal National Lifeboat Institution, Mrs Heather Deane, assistant public relations officer, R.N.L.I., the Pembrokeshire Record Office of Dyfed Archives, Regional Librarian Mr J. I. Davies and his staff at Haverfordwest, Mr Robert Kennedy, curator of Pembrokeshire Museums, Mr Wilfred Harrison, M.B.E., honorary curator Tenby Museum, the Public Record Office, the National Maritime Museum, the Hydrographic Department, Ministry of Defence, Trinity House Lighthouse Service, and Eric Freeman, author of *The Solva Saga*, for permission to reproduce part of The Ballad of the Phoebe and Peggy.

I also acknowledge the help I have received from so many sources with photographs and illustrations, particularly the R.N.L.I., National Maritime Museum, Tenby Museum, Western Telegraph, Studio Jon, Mr Martin Cavaney, Mr Malcolm Richards and Mr Norman Mabe, former hon. secretary of the Fishguard Lifeboat.

Special thanks are extended to Mr Lynn Hughes and my publishers, and to my wife and daughter for 'sailing' with me through the perils of the deep.

To Doris and Karen

Contents

List of Illustrations

Storm Force

The great storm of 1703 was one of the worst ever to hit the coast of Britain. Over 150 ships were wrecked and about 8,000 people lost their lives during the two days — November 26th and 27th. Pembrokeshire escaped relatively lightly. Many of the ships off the coastline had already reached shelter when the south-easterly gale veered to the north-west, bringing with it a violent storm.

But even vessels which had sailed into port felt the effects of this weather disaster. Britain was at war with France and a huge convoy of 130 merchantmen had been shepherded into Milford Haven by Her Majesty's ships *Dolphin, Cumberland, Coventry, Looe, Hastings* and *Hector*, under the command of Captain Josiah Soanes. The storm reached its height at about three in

The 'Nightingale' being deserted by her crew in the breakers at Lydstep Bay.
(From a Charles Norris watercolour in the Tenby Museum collection).

the morning of the 27th. The *Cumberland* broke her sheet anchor and was driven close to the *Dolphin* and the Haven-based *H.M.S. Rye.*

'She drove very near the rocks,' wrote Soanes afterwards, 'having but one anchor left, but in a little time they slung a gun, with the broken anchor fast to it, which they let go and wonderfully preserved the ship from the shore.

'Guns firing from one ship or other all night for help, though 'twas impossible to assist each other, the sea was so high and the darkness of the night such, that we could not see where any one was, but by the flashes of the guns.

'When daylight appeared, it was a dismal sight to behold the ships driving up and down, one foul of another, without masts, some sunk, and others upon the rocks, the wind blowing so hard, with thunder, lightning and rain, that on the deck a man could not stand without holding.'

Some ships, it was reported, were driven from the shelter of the Haven village of Dale and "split into pieces" with the loss of all on board. Others were driven high on to the shore and one was swept ten miles along the port before she could be anchored.

'A ketch of Pembroke,' said Soanes, 'was drove on to rocks. The two men and boy in her had no boat to save their lives, but in this great distress a boat which broke from another ship drove by them, without any in her. The two men leaped into her and were saved, but the boy was drowned.'

At Pembroke itself, a prize ship was lifted on to the town's Mill Bridge.

The storm continued until three in the afternoon, with 30 ships wrecked and three missing. Such were the perils faced by the eighteenth century mariner. For in great storms even the superb anchorage of Milford Haven was not secure. But the seamen who survived were thankful not to have been caught out at sea off one of the most dangerous stretches of coastline in the world. Pembrokeshire is at the crossroads of some of the busiest shipping routes and its waters are the graveyard of thousands of vessels caught in distress. From the earliest times, men and women have died on the county's treacherous shores. Even the sophisticated navigation aids of today are no sure guarantee of safety on the high seas and the boom in the tourist industry is reflected in the number of small boat tragedies which occur in inshore waters each year.

The First and Second World Wars also took a particularly heavy toll on shipping and Milford Haven was an important convoy assembly point in both conflicts. The Haven has been receiving the trading ships of the world for centuries and there is evidence of medieval lights having been sited on St Ann's Head to guide ships to safety.

Trinity House approved two coal-fired lights there in the seventeenth century, although when it was discovered that the owners were obtaining dues illegally, the lights were closed down. It was 40 years before they were re-kindled and there has been a lighthouse on the headland — at one time there were two — ever since.

The most famous of the Pembrokeshire lights is on the Smalls — a group of deadly rocks 17 miles off the mainland. The first proposal to build a lighthouse there was made in 1774 and within two years the light was burning — with the resultant saving of many lives. At one time, the Smalls was the most lucrative lighthouse in the world and when Trinity House was empowered to

The Smalls lighthouse which warns mariners of the deadly group of rocks off the Pembrokeshire coast. When the sea is rough the rocks are completely submerged. The present lighthouse was built in 1861.

(Picture: Martin Cavaney).

take over control of all lights in 1836, they had to pay its owner £170,000 in compensation!

An incident on the Smalls one winter led to three men, instead of two, being appointed to man isolated rock lights. The two keepers there were cut off by storms for four months and one of them died. His companion feared that if he threw the body into the sea, he would be accused of murder, so he lashed it to the gallery outside the lantern room. Relief ships approached the lighthouse, but were unable to land, and marvelled that the solitary figure in the gallery was able to watch them for so long in the storm and intense cold. When the lighthouse was finally reached, the man on the gallery was found to be a corpse and the ordeal had broken the other keeper's health. But he was commended for faithfully keeping the light burning despite the circumstance and the hardships.

By 1840, two more lighthouses had been established off the coastline — on Caldey Island (1829) and South Bishop Rock (1839). Lights were built on Strumble Head in 1908 and on Skokholm Island in 1916.

Skokholm Lighthouse on a bird sanctuary island off the Pembrokeshire coast. The lighthouse was established in 1916.

The only lightship to have been stationed in Pembrokeshire waters marks shoals which lie three miles off St Govan's Head. There has been a lightvessel there since 1907. These were the official lights, but there were those who hung out false lights to lure ships on to rocks. Merchantmen foundering were speedily plundered before Coastguards and Customs officers could reach the scene.

The title 'Coastguard' was first used officially in 1822, when orders were issued

The Trinity House Lightvessel 'St. Gowan', which marks shoals three miles off St. Govan's Head. (Picture: Martin Cavaney).

that 'the whole of the forces for the prevention of smuggling' should be consolidated under the Board of Customs. By the 1850s — as the smuggling boom began to wane — the coastguard service turned more and more to life-saving and coast-watching activities and in 1856 it came under the control of the Admiralty. The service retained quasi-naval status right up to 1925, when it became the peacetime responsibility of the Board of Trade. This mutlifarious organisation's tasks now include search and rescue, the location and guarding of wrecks, weather reporting and the disposal of 'Fishes Royal', such as sturgeon. Coastguards alert rescue services, such as lifeboats and RAF helicopters in Pembrokeshire, assist holidaymakers trapped on the county's cliffs or cut off by the tide and bring animals trapped on rocky ledges to safety. Its headquarters in Pembrokeshire is at St Ann's Head — the maritime rescue sub-centre which in an emergency is also the base for pollution

A Whirlwind HAR 10 helicopter of 22 Squadron, RAF Brawdy, on exercise with St. David's Life-Boat in the 1970s. (Picture: Western Telegraph).

The search and rescue role of the RAF portrayed by a Nimrod long-range maritime patrol aircraft, a Westland Sea King helicopter and a Seal class marine craft on a training exercise. (Picture: RAF).

operations control. Other Coastguard stations are strategically located along the coastline.

The massive increase in sea trade in the eighteenth and nineteenth centuries was reflected in the number of wrecks off Pembrokeshire. But when the Royal National Institution for the Preservation of Life from Shipwreck was founded in 1824, there was only one lifeboat on this coastline — at Fishguard. In 1852, a station was established at Tenby by the Shipwrecked Mariners' Society and two years later it was handed over to the Royal National Lifeboat Institution. Angle lifeboat station was opened in 1868, and St David's a year later. There have been lifeboats at these four points ever since and they have saved a total of over 1,300 lives. Lifeboat stations were also set up by the R.N.L.I. at Solva, in 1869; Little Haven, in 1882; and Newport in 1884, but by 1895 only Little Haven was still open. It, too, was finally closed in 1921, after a long record of heroic service, but in 1967 an inshore lifeboat station was established at Little Haven. There is also an inshore lifeboat at Tenby, an indication of the increase

in boating and bathing accidents off the resort in the last two decades.

Pembrokeshire's first lifeboats were powered by oars and sail, with a coxswain, second coxswain, bowman and between eight and ten men at the oars. In 1908, a £3,298 steam lifeboat — the *James Stevens 3* — was sent to Angle. She broke away from her moorings in 1915, however, and was badly damaged when she drifted onto rocks. She was later withdrawn from the station and replaced by a succession of oared boats. Angle finally got its first motor lifeboat, the *Elizabeth Elson*, in 1929. Fishguard had received a motor lifeboat 20 years before. The *Charterhouse*, built at a cost of £2,948, was the gift of 'old and present' Cathusians. St David's first motor lifeboat was the *General Farrell*, which went into service in 1912. But Tenby had to wait until 1923 before it received the *John R. Webb* — the first cabin lifeboat to be completed for the R.N.L.I. — whose six-cylinder engine gave her a speed of eight knots in all weathers.

Members of Pembrokeshire's Life-Saving Apparatus Companies also played their part in rescuing shipwrecked sailors from cliffs or rocks inaccessible to the lifeboats. Many hundreds of lives were saved by these companies, using first mortar and later rocket apparatus to fire a line to a wreck so that survivors could be hauled to safety in a breeches buoy.

The Royal Navy and the RAF have assumed a major role in rescue operations on Pembrokeshire's coast in recent years. First Naval, and now RAF, helicopters stationed at Brawdy have flown on hundreds of rescue missions. Some have involved oil tankers, which arrive in their thousands each year at Milford Haven — now the second largest oil port in Europe. Despite stringent safeguards, oil pollution is an ever-present danger to the county's magnificent coastline and when a tanker hits the headlines, all Pembrokeshire holds its breath!

The collier brig 'Durham' wrecked at Saundersfoot on February 23rd, 1839.
(From a Charles Norris watercolour in the Tenby Museum collection).

The Fishguard Life-Boat 'Charterhouse', which went to the aid of the Dutch motor schooner 'Hermina' in December, 1920. The 'Charterhouse' served at Fishguard from 1909-1930 and saved a total of 47 lives. (Picture: Studio Jon).

Lifeboat V.C.

Coxswain John Howells was already in his sixties when in 1920 he became the only Pembrokeshire lifeboatman ever to win the Lifeboat V.C. — the gold medal of the Royal National Lifeboat Institution. On a cold and clear Thursday afternoon in December the Dutch motor schooner *Hermina* left her mooring at Fishguard Harbour, bound for Rotterdam. She had been sheltering at the port for some days, but now that the weather conditions had improved, Captain Vooitgedacht and his crew of nine were hoping to be back in Holland in time for the New Year celebrations.

That night, however, the wind freshened until it was blowing a moderate gale from the north-west and the *Hermina* was compelled to return to Fishguard, where she anchored outside the breakwater. During the daylight hours of December 3rd, the wind increased and as darkness set in, the *Hermina* was riding heavily to her anchors. As the schooner's situation worsened,

Captain Vooitgedacht grew increasingly concerned for their safety and at 6.40 p.m. ordered distress flares to be fired. Coastguards at once alerted Fishguard's lifeboat, the *Charterhouse*, and at 7.15 p.m. she was heading, under motor power, across the bay to the schooner. By the time the lifeboat reached her, the *Hermina* had dragged her anchors for a considerable distance and was grinding heavily on rocks in tremendous seas.

Coxswain Howells anchored the lifeboat to windward of the stricken ship and veered down to her. Only with the greatest difficulty and at great risk, was he able to get ropes on board the schooner. The sea was lifting the lifeboat right into the ship's rigging, which at one stage prevented her from being dashed down on to the *Hermina*'s deck. Despite the conditions, the lifeboat managed to take seven of the schooner's crew off safely, but the captain, chief officer and second mate refused to leave. Coxswain Howells implored them to

23

Life-Boat V.C. Coxswain John Howells – awarded the R.N.L.I. gold medal for the heroic service to the Dutch motor schooner 'Hermina' in December, 1920.
(Picture: R.N.L.I.).

Second Coxswain Thomas Oakley Davies, of the Fishguard Life-Boat 'Charterhouse'. He was awarded the R.N.L.I. silver medal for the 'Hermina' rescue in 1920.
(Picture: R.N.L.I.).

Motor Mechanic Robert E. Simpson, of the Fishguard Life-Boat 'Charterhouse' . . . also awarded the R.N.L.I. silver medal for the 'Hermina' service.
(Picture: R.N.L.I.).

Lifeboatman Thomas Holmes, of the Fishguard Life-Boat 'Charterhouse' . . . third member of the crew to receive the R.N.L.I. silver medal for the 'Hermina' service.
(Picture: R.N.L.I.).

change their minds. It would be impossible for the lifeboat to return, he said, and very soon the *Hermina* would be smashed to pieces, with the rising tide, on the cliffs at Needle Rock. Still they refused to heed his pleas and the lifeboat prepared to return to Fishguard without them, on a journey which was to test the skill and courage of her coxswain and crew — because, while the rescue was being carried out, the motor mechanic, Robert Simpson, discovered the lifeboat was leaking. Despite his repeated efforts, in very difficult conditions, the engine refused to start.

The lifeboat was now caught under sheer cliffs in the face of a whole gale, yet magnificent seamanship on the part of the coxswain, the readiest obedience of the crew and courageous determination, was to see them all safely home that night. Coxswain Howells knew that their only chance was to sail the waterlogged lifeboat out. But no sooner had he cast off, than the mizzen sail was blown to ribbons, became unhooked and was lost overboard. This left only the main sail set. Their position seemed hopeless. But in response to their coxswain's call,

second coxswain Tom Davies and lifeboatman Tom Holmes crawled out on to the forward end box and with great seas breaking over them, they succeeded in setting the jib sail. Their prompt action saved the lifeboat and all on board.

At midnight, three hours after leaving the wreck, the lifeboat reached Fishguard under sail and oars. They had been on shore for only a short time, when flares were again sent up from the schooner, but it was now impossible for the lifeboat to return. The fight to save the lives of the three men still on board the schooner rested with the crew of the rocket apparatus — already in position on the cliff top above Needle Rock.

Captain Vooitgedacht and the chief officer succeeded in reaching rocks and were both hauled to safety, but the third mate was washed away and drowned. The survivors were completely exhausted by their ordeal and one of the rocket apparatus crew, William Morgan, had to go down the cliffs for the chief officer, who was lying on a ledge with the waves breaking over him. In his report of the *Hermina* service, the honorary secretary of Fishguard Lifeboat,

M. L. Nicholls, wrote: 'It is admitted by all concerned and by many old lifeboatmen that the Fishguard Lifeboat had never been in such a perilous and anxious position in her history.'

On December 17th, the committee of management of the R.N.L.I. decided that the circumstances of the rescue and the skill and courage shown were of so exceptional a character as to justify the award of their highest honour to Coxswain Howells — the gold medal. For their special services, second coxswain Tom Davies; motor mechanic Bob Simpson and lifeboatman Tom Holmes were awarded silver medals. The crew had shown exceptional courage and resolution in carrying out the orders of their coxswain and bronze medals were awarded to lifeboatmen T. Perkins, J. Rourke, P. Whelan, T. Duffin, J. Gardiner, W. Devereux, H. W. Mason, W. Thomas and R. Veal. Each member of the crew was also voted an additional monetary reward. William Morgan, of the rocket apparatus crew, received the Thanks of the Institution on Vellum, in recognition of his courageous action in rescuing the *Hermina*'s chief officer. He was also given the same monetary reward as the lifeboat crew. Coxswain Howells' gold medal was the first awarded by the R.N.L.I. for three years and in April, 1921, he and his crew travelled to London ro receive their awards from the Prince of Wales.

The Dutch Shipping Board, which sat to examine the causes of the loss of the schooner, expressed its 'great admiration of the courage and seamanship of the coxswain and all his crew'. On the first anniversary of the rescue, the Queen of the Netherlands and the Dutch Government showed their appreciation of the service by presenting gold watches to Coxswain Howells and William Morgan and silver watches to the lifeboatmen. Coxswain Howells was over 70 and had retired from the Institution's service when in 1924 he returned to London to receive the Empire Gallantry Medal from King George V at Buckingham Palace. He was one of eight living holders of the gold medal to be specially honoured by the King in that centenary year of the R.N.L.I. The following year — on March 14th, 1925 — Coxswain Howells died and Pembrokeshire mourned the death of the county's first 'Lifeboat V.C.'.

Less than 15 years earlier, the little community of St David's had itself been in mourning when disaster overtook its lifeboat with the loss of three lives. The *Gem* — a twelve-oared sailing and pulling lifeboat — had cost £390 and was provided for the station under the legacy of John Metcalfe, of York. This lifeboat had been at St David's for 25 years, when on October 12th, 1910, she went to the aid of the Barnstaple ketch *Democrat*. She was a Milford-built ketch, commanded by Captain Tom Welch, and had been sheltering in Ramsey Sound in a moderate north-north-easterly gale with her two anchors down. As the prevailing gale increased, Captain Welch feared that his anchors would drag and made signals for assistance. The St David's Lifeboat crew assembled at their St Justinian station and the *Gem* was launched in darkness over the stone slipway into heavy seas. It was blowing a full gale with occasional showers, as the fifty-seven year old coxswain, John Stephens, set a course for the *Democrat*, his crew straining at the oars in the wild waters of the Sound.

After two unsuccessful attempts, the lifeboat got alongside the ketch, which was now dangerously close to the reef of rocks known as the Bitches — black stumps protruding treacherously from the foaming white sea. Captain Welch and his crew of two were taken on board the lifeboat and Coxswain Stephens gave orders to sheer off. The crew fought desperately at the oars, but were unable to straighten the lifeboat's head up against the wind, sea and tide. The boat was being swept rapidly towards the Bitches and the coxswain, knowing it was impossible to pull clear, decided to try and take it through a narrow passage in the reef. In the darkness, this one route to safety was only discernible by its foam and, as the lifeboat headed for the gap, it struck a rock, throwing all on board into the 'boiling mad' sea.

Fifteen men, including the captain and crew of the *Democrat*, succeeded in reaching the Bitches. But Coxswain Stephens and lifeboatmen Henry Rowlands and James Price were swept away and drowned. The *Gem* was last seen drifting away into the night and was totally wrecked. Nothing was known of the tragedy on the mainland

The St. David's Life-Boat 'Gem', lost in Ramsey Sound in October, 1910.

(Picture: R.N.L.I.).

until about nine in the morning, when one of the survivors managed to burn some oilskins to attract attention.

The seas still raged through Ramsey Sound and there was no sign of the storm abating. The plight of those on the Bitches looked hopeless, but a young fisherman, Sydney Mortimer, called for volunteers to go out to the reef. Coastguardmen Sam Guppy and Sam Husk promptly responded and the three set off for Porthclais Harbour, on the other side of the headland, to launch a 20-foot shore boat, the *Wave Queen*.

Fifty years after the 'Gem' disaster . . . Sydney Mortimer on the cliffs overlooking Ramsey Sound where the St. David's Life-Boat came to grief in October, 1910, with the loss of her coxswain and two crew members. Across the Sound are the deadly Bitches rocks and the island of Ramsey.

Brave Sydney Mortimer – at 18½, the youngest life-boat coxswain in the British Isles.

When their boat reached the entrance to the Sound, it was struck by a squall which carried away part of the rigging and half-filled the craft with water. The rest of the rigging was cut free and, while the coast-guards baled, Mortimer rowed with the yoke steering lines tied to his legs. The seas around the Bitches were too rough for them to approach and the men on the reef were too exhausted by exposure and their ordeal for any attempt to be made to haul them through the water to the *Wave Queen*.

Mortimer decided he would stand by until the tide had fallen and, four hours later, he took five men off the rocks and landed them on Ramsey Island. He then returned and took five more ashore and was going back for a third time when another shore boat, manned by Eleazer James and four others, hove into view and took off the remaining survivors.

Fishguard's new lifeboat, the *Charterhouse*, had been alerted earlier by telegraph and battled 16 miles through mountainous seas to help their comrades in distress. When she arrived in the Sound, the fifteen survivors had already been taken off

The memorial at St. David's Cathedral Cemetery to Coxswain John Stephens and lifeboatmen Henry Rowlands and James Price, who lost their lives in October, 1910, when disaster overtook the St. David's Life-Boat 'Gem', in the wild waters of Ramsey Sound. (Picture: John Evans).

the reef. The boat of Eleazer James was in imminent danger of being swamped, however, and the lifeboat gave them a line and towed the craft to safety. The survivors from the *Gem* and *Democrat* were landed on the mainland. Many of them were in a state of collapse and in need of medical attention. The bodies of Coxswain Stephens and the two lifeboatmen were recovered from the shore on Ramsey and brought back to St Justinian the next day — 40 hours after the gallant *Gem* had set out on her last rescue mission.

Coxswain Stephens and Henry Rowlands were both married and the R.N.L.I. voted £100 to each of their widows and £25 to Rowlands' dependent daughter. A local fund raised £300. Sydney Mortimer's heroic

Sydney Mortimer with the 12 survivors of the St. David's Life-Boat 'Gem'.

31

conduct was recognised by the R.N.L.I. with the award of its silver medal. The Institution's Thanks on Vellum went to Sam Guppy and Sam Husk, who also received Board of Trade silver medals. Monetary awards were made to all three by the R.N.L.I., who also voted pecuniary rewards to Eleazer James and the crew of the other shore boat, and to the coxswain and crew of the Fishguard Lifeboat. Mortimer later received the Sea Gallantry Medal from King George V at a Buckingham Palace investiture; a cash award from the Carnegie Hero Fund, and engraved silver binoculars from the Government, but perhaps the highest tribute paid to him was that he was appointed coxswain of St David's Lifeboat — at eighteen-and-a-half the youngest lifeboat coxswain in the British Isles.

The ketch *Democrat* survived that October storm and the following January figured in a second rescue operation — this time in Fishguard Bay. She was one of a number of vessels, from which crews were taken off by the Fishguard Lifeboat *Charterhouse* in a violent gale. The bravery of Mortimer, Guppy and Husk was subsequently commemorated in a ballad by George Ashurst.

THE BALLAD OF 'BITCHES ROCK'

The booming gun rang out its knell across the wave-swept bay;
'Twas midnight and midst the cottage homes sweet sleep held gentle sway.
The sleepers woke, then bade farewell to sobbing babes and wives,
While spray and foam and shrieking wind screamed peril to their lives.

At danger's call, they forced their way against the thund'ring wind,
And struggled t'wards the lifeboat house perchance a tomb to find.
But well they knew 'neath blackest night, where surging waters waved,
Were human souls in jeopardy, who for their mercy craved.

The boat was launched, it trembled 'neath the shock of raging sea,
The groaning oars they creaked and bent, firm gripped by Britons free.
And at their head was Stephens brave, with dauntless nerve and brain;
Cold was the wind, yea, icy cold. It cut and lashed in vain.

They reached the wreck and saved the crew, then turned to make for port,
But now the sea, the baffled sea, with fury was distraught,
By mountain floods, she drove them back upon the Bitches Rock,
'Ha! Ha!,' she laughed in bitter scorn, 'Dar'st thou my rage to mock?'

The boat stove in upon the rocks, now swept by wind and tide,
And all essayed to save their lives by climbing up the side.
Drenched by the foam, they huddled close to stave off the flowing sea,
And thought of those they'd left at home across there on the lea.

Their oilskin coats they torches made, and shouted loud their plight,
But never answ'ring call came back, the wind laughed in its flight.
And death stared at them out the foam, and vainly tried to seize
Those stalwart sons so full of life, its hunger to appease.

And on the land their trembling wives searched for them through the night,
And saw the flares that mournful beamed across the tempest's might.
Then dark despair came on the town and grief like mist o'erspread,
'No boat could live in such a sea,' experienced seamen said.

'Who'll join with me?' cried Mortimer, 'those billows wild to brave,
I cannot leave them to their fate without attempt to save.'
'We'll join with you,' the coastguard cried, 'We'll give a helping hand,
'Tis desperate, but we'll try our best to bring them to the land.'

Then daring men 'gainst Nature's might rowed out their little boat,
Husk, Guppy, Mortimer, the crew, those heroes' names to quote.
They dragged their comrades from the rocks and brought them safe to shore,
To wailing wives, borne down with grief, their loved ones to restore.

My hand to you brave Mortimer! A lesson you have taught,
That courage, nobleness, is not alone with luxury wrought.
Amidst the poor, the lowly born, they shine with brightest ray,
And show the glimmer of the soul embedded in its clay.

In 1956, tragedy struck the community at St David's, when a member of the lifeboat crew, Ieuan Bateman, was lost overboard. The lifeboat, *Swˆn-y-mˆor*, was making for Milford Haven after rescuing eight Frenchmen from the *Notre Dame de Fatima* on November 8th, when she was submerged by following waves off St Ann's Head. Ieuan Bateman was washed out of the boat and his body was recovered two days later at West Dale. The French Government post-humously awarded him the Life-Saving Silver Medal, 1st class, and the French Life-boat Society voted him the bronze medal and diploma. The lifeboat's coxswain, Dai Lewis, received the R.N.L.I. bronze medal for this difficult rescue, which was made with skill, courage and resource in severe and dangerous conditions.

The ill-fated *Gem* was replaced by a temporary lifeboat and in 1911, St David's received its first motor lifeboat, the *General Farrell*, built at a cost of £3,003. The *General Farrell* remained at this station for twenty-four years and in 1929, together with Angle Lifeboat, it featured in a rescue which became world-wide news.

The thirty year old cargo ship, *Molesey*, left Manchester, in ballast, for Cardiff on Sunday, November 24th, under the command of Captain G. E. Huntley. She carried a crew of thirty three, together with two women passengers and the wife of the first officer, W. H. Stocks. Hours after leaving port, the 3,809-ton steamship ran into a 70 mph gale, which gave her a severe battering. The *Molesey* ploughed on into the night, but in the early hours of Monday morning, when off St David's Head, she broke a propeller and was left in a perilous position in one of the worst storms for many years. Her S.O.S. was picked up by Fishguard Radio, which informed Tenby Coastguard that the ship was drifting towards rocks at Skokholm Island. As the storm had blown down the telephone and telegraph lines between Tenby and Pembroke, the message to Angle Lifeboat had to be taken part of the way by car. It took nearly two hours for news of her distress signal to reach the honorary secretary of Angle Lifeboat, A. William Gutch. The new motor lifeboat *Elizabeth Elson* was launched, and she met the full

The Angle Life-Boat 'Elizabeth Elson', which went to the aid of the steamship 'Molesey' in November, 1929. The 'Elizabeth Elson' served at Angle from 1929-1957 and saved a total of 144 lives. (Picture: Beken & Son).

force of the south-westerly gale as she rounded St Ann's Head and made for Skokholm. A thorough search was made in the vicinity of the island, but nothing was found, and two hours later the lifeboat was back at Milford Haven.

Naturalist Ronald Lockley — who was then farming Skokholm — had been stranded on the mainland by the storm, unable to reach his island home. It was nearing dusk when he saw the *Molesey* ashore on the south-east side of Midland — a tiny island between Skomer and the Marloes peninsula. This new information was given to the coastguards and at 7.45 on that Monday evening, the Angle Lifeboat went out again — battling through heavy seas to reach the *Molesey*. Visibility was barely 70 yards and although Coxswain James Watkins took his boat so close to the little island that the breakers could be seen, no ship could be distinguished. He wisely decided to return to Milford Haven to await daylight. He and his crew had been at sea for four hours, but soon after six on the Tuesday morning they set out again and this time the stricken steamship was located.

The lifeboat anchored and succeeded in manoeuvring alongside the wreck, but the task of taking off those on board proved very difficult and extremely dangerous. The wind was blowing against the tide and the lifeboat was rising and falling up to 20 feet in the seas, with submerged rocks to either side of her. But, in an hour-long operation, the twenty-eight survivors were taken off, including two women and a man with both legs broken. Six crew members and the wife of the chief officer had been lost in mountainous seas soon after the ship hit the rocks.

A number of Marloes fishermen had rowed out at daybreak across the murderous waters of Jack Sound to reach the *Molesey*. As they closed on the wreck, they saw the Angle Lifeboat coming up from the south and knew it would be better for this much larger craft to take off all the survivors in one operation. The lifeboat reached Milford Haven at 11 a.m. and after landing the *Molesey*'s crew and the two passengers, she returned to her station. The St David's Lifeboat had also been launched the previous night, but Coxswain Ivor Arnold and his

Some of the crew of the cargo ship 'Molesey' rescued by the Angle Life-Boat 'Elizabeth Elson' in November, 1929.
(Picture: R.N.L.I.).

crew had met difficulties even before the craft hit the waters of Ramsey Sound. The road linking the lifeboat station with St David's was under water and lifeboat honorary secretary, Dr Joseph Soar, had to battle through the floods in his car with the coxswain and crew.

It was midnight when the lifeboat, the *General Farrell* got away, and she faced huge seas in St Bride's Bay. She reached the position of the wreck at 2.30 a.m. and burned flares without response. Nothing could be seen of the ship in the darkness and Coxswain Arnold — like the Angle coxswain — decided to resume the search at daybreak. As the heavy seas and frequent squalls made it impossible to wait in the neighbourhood of Skomer, he put into Milford Haven for shelter. The Angle Lifeboat was also waiting there, but without radio the two lifeboats remained out of touch.

At daylight, the St David's boat again went in search of the *Molesey*. When he found her, Coxswain Arnold knew he had been close to her when he fired the flares which had brought no response from the ship. But by now, the survivors had already been taken off by the Angle boat and Coxswain Arnold and his crew battled their way back across St Bride's Bay. When they reached their station, they had been at sea for some twelve hours.

Ronald Lockley, who had been with the Marloes fishermen who put out to the rescue, returned to his Skokholm Island the next day. As his boat passed the wreck of the *Molesey*, he and his companion heard a weak call from near the ship. A Maltese fireman, Paola Attard, who had remained hidden on board during the rescue operation and was believed drowned, had managed to reach rocks on Midland. Lockley took his boat alongside the island and the ship's last survivor was brought to safety.

Coxswain Watkins, of Angle, was later awarded the R.N.L.I.'s bronze medal in recognition of his judgement, perseverance and fine seamanship. The motor mechanic, Edgar Rees, was voted the Thanks of the Institution on Vellum for his efficient handling of the lifeboat's engines throughout the service. Thanks on Vellum also went to lifeboat secretary, William

Gutch, who had done everything possible to obtain information and, although not a seaman, he accompanied the lifeboat on the third and successful search. Similar Thanks were voted to Coxswain Arnold, of St David's, for his good judgement and fine seamanship. Letters of appreciation were sent to the crews of both lifeboats and to Dr Joseph Soar, like Mr Gutch also not a seaman, who had accompanied the lifeboat on its service. O. T. Evans, foreman of works to R.N.L.I. engineers, was also thanked for going out with the lifeboat. The Institution paid tribute to the Marloes fishermen for their brave part in the rescue and to the village postmaster for passing messages during the operation. The attention of the Board of Trade was drawn to the help received from the divisional officer of Coastguard at Tenby and the men under his command. The owners of the *Molesey*, Messrs Watts, Watts and Company — the Britain Steamship Company — sent a donation of £105 to the R.N.L.I. 'as some small recognition of the fine work done by the Angle and St David's motor lifeboats'. They also sent £20 to the Marloes fishermen. A final accolade came from the Pembrokeshire County Council, who passed a formal resolution recording its 'high appreciation of the gallantry of the crews of lifeboats stationed in the county and of the gallantry of the fishermen of Marloes'.

Nine years later came another outstanding rescue when eight men were snatched to safety in as many seconds by Tenby's Lifeboat, the *John R. Webb*, when the Belfast coaster *Fermanagh* — bound, light, from the Irish port of Drogheda to Llanelli — had run for the shelter of Caldey Roads in a south-westerly gale. During that day — Friday, January 14th, 1938 — she attempted to resume her voyage. The weather conditions forced her to return, however, and she again dropped anchor in the Roads. Later that night the wind increased, with frequent gusts at hurricane force, and the seas were so rough they were breaking right over St Catherine's Fort perched high on the island just off the mainland at Tenby. Rain and driving spray made visibility very poor. The *Fermanagh* was rolling heavily in the swell and soon began dragging her anchors. First one cable parted and then the other and the ship was left drifting helplessly towards the deadly Woolhouse Rocks about a mile-and-a-half offshore. Distress signals were fired and the lifeboat was alerted by the Tenby Coastguard at about 4.30 in the morning. By 5.15 a.m., she was forging through the heavy seas with second coxswain John Rees in command — the coxswain being away from the station.

When the lifeboat reached the *Fermanagh*, she was already aground on Woolhouse on an even keel. But the coaster

The Tenby Life-Boat 'John R. Webb' – second boat of that name to be stationed at Tenby. She served at the seaside resort from 1930-1955 and saved a total of 53 lives, including eight crew members from the 'Fermanagh' in January, 1938.
(Picture: R.N.L.I.).

then came clear of the rocks and drifted before the gale — her stern sinking, her bows in the air and her decks awash. Acting coxswain Rees could see men on board the ship and with great skill he took the lifeboat alongside. She was there for just eight seconds, but in that time the *Fermanagh*'s crew of eight were able to leap to safety. The coaster's master was not among them. Before the lifeboat arrived he had launched the ship's boat and had clambered on board to fend the craft off while his crew followed. As he did so, the rope snapped and the boat was swept away. The lifeboat had already searched around the *Fermanagh* as she lay on the rocks and had seen nothing of the master. She now returned to Tenby with the exhausted survivors and put out again in a renewed, but unsuccessful, bid to find him.

Shortly before 11 that morning, the lifeboat returned to Tenby. The weather was so bad that the boat could not be re-housed until late in the afternoon and the crew remained on board, taking it in turns to go ashore for food. The lifeboat crew had been severely shaken in the heavy seas while on service. During the five-and-a-half hours they had been out at sea, they had been in continual danger of being washed overboard and two of them were nearly lost when the lifeboat dropped into a deep trough. Acting coxswain Rees had handled the lifeboat with skill and courage. He had acted with great promptness when he saw that the *Fermanagh* had drifted off the rocks and was liable to founder at any minute. For his gallantry, he was awarded the R.N.L.I. silver medal and the lifeboat's motor mechanic Alfred Cottam received the bronze medal. Each of the other seven members of the crew — Fred Harries, Thomas E. Lewis, Frank Hooper, Alexander Harries, Bertie Lewis, Henry Thomas and James N. Crockford — received the Institution's Thanks on Vellum.

The North Coast

North Pembrokeshire's rugged coastline from Cemaes Head to St David's Head, with the great mass of Strumble Head thrusting its way into the sea between them, has witnessed the death of hundreds of ships. Even vessels which sought shelter in Fishguard Bay could be in peril in gales from a foul quarter.

Two smacks, the *John and Grace*, of Milford, and the *Mary*, of Cardigan, were driven onto Goodwick Sands in November, 1872, after their cables parted in a violent gale from the north-east. The

Sailing vessels beached on Goodwick Sands after a storm in the early 1900s.

(Picture: Studio Jon).

Fishguard Lifeboat, the *Sir Edward Perrott*, was launched and rescued four men from the wrecked smacks. Scarcely had the lifeboat crew had time to change their clothing, when they had to launch again to save the crews of three more small vessels driven on to the sands.

Three years later — again in a November north-easterly storm — distress signals were hoisted by a number of ships at anchor in Fishguard Roads and the lifeboat saved 16 lives. The schooner *Elinor and Mary* parted her cables and was swept onto Goodwick Sands, with breakers sweeping her fore and aft. Three men were taken off her in a daring rescue and landed safely. The lifeboat then went out to the Caernarvon smack *Laura* and took her crew off. Soon afterwards, the schooner *Independence* parted her cables and was driven before the gale on to the beach. She was overwhelmed by the huge seas and when the lifeboat reached her, the crew of three were clinging to the rigging. One by one the survivors were brought off the wreck, but the lifeboatmen still had more seamen to save that day.

The Cardigan schooner, *Princess Royal*, was also stranded on the sands and her crew lashed themselves to the rigging to avoid being swept overboard. All were taken off by the lifeboat and in recognition of this gallant rescue, the Fishguard coxswain, James White, was voted a second clasp to the silver medal he had previously been awarded by the R.N.L.I.

In 1877, Coxswain White won his third silver award, while in command of Fishguard's No. 2 lifeboat, the *Fraser*. For their own safety, the crews of the New York brigantine *B. F. Nash* and the Bridgwater schooner *Adventure* had been taken off their vessels in a heavy gale on February 20th. But on the 23rd, the gale swung to the north-east, increased in fury and whipped up tremendous seas in Fishguard Bay. The crews had by this time returned to their ships and the *B. F. Nash* was driven down on to the sands. Signals of distress were sighted from three vessels at anchor — the smack *George Evans*, of Newquay; the *Adventure* and the Newport schooner, *Supply*. The lifeboat rescued the crews of all three ships and then returned to the aid of the *B. F. Nash*. Soon after the lifeboat reached her, the tide

One of the early Fishguard Life-Boats, the 'Elizabeth Mary', which served at the port from 1889-1907.   (Picture: R.N.L.I.).

44

ebbed and the crew decided to stay with the ship.

On one occasion — November 16th, 1882 — the Fishguard Lifeboat was launched no fewer than five times in the same day in a fresh north-north-easterly gale and saved forty-six people from fifteen different vessels.

When the Royal National Lifeboat Institution took over the Fishguard station in 1855, there had been a lifeboat at the port for at least 33 years. One of the earliest recorded rescues was in October, 1825, when a two-masted vessel, *Horatio*, was wrecked in Fishguard Bay. Her crew of six scrambled on to rocks and were guided up the cliff to safety. Seven lives were saved from the schooner *Trevor* which foundered in a gale in 1836 between Saddle Point and Goodwick Sands. And in 1849, the silver medal of the Royal National Institution for the Preservation of Life from Shipwreck — forerunner of the R.N.L.I. — was awarded to William Rees. Rees commanded a shore boat which saved all those on board the Gloucester brig *Lady Kenmare*, which was wrecked on Goodwick Sands.

Newport (Pembs.) — some miles further along the coast — was the setting of another 'silver' rescue. On March 17th, 1863, the Cardigan sloop *Francis* was swept before a northerly gale on to the local sands. Ferocious seas roared over the ship and the crew of three were in great danger of being washed overboard to their deaths. Two local men, George Lewis and Thomas Rowlands waded out as far as they dared into the foaming breakers and managed to hurl a line to the little sloop, which by now had almost disappeared. The line was secured and the three crewmen were hauled to the shore. For their bravery, Rowlands and Lewis received R.N.L.I. silver medals.

In 1884, the Institution established a lifeboat station at Newport, but in ten years it had only three service calls and saved 11 lives.

The lifeboat's last launch on service was in the darkness of a wild October night in 1889, when the brigantine *Reliance*, of Wexford, had her masts carried away in a full gale. The lifeboat was pounded by heavy seas as she put out and was in considerable danger as Coxswain William James skilfully brought her alongside the wreck. Three of the ship's crew of four were brought off, but the extreme conditions prevented the lifeboat returning to her station. She was now forced to head for Cardigan, where the three survivors were landed safely. The fourth member of the brigantine's crew had been washed overboard before the lifeboat could reach the ship.

The St David's lifeboat station was established in 1869 at the request of local people and the initial services of the new lifeboat, *Augusta*, were in October and November of the following year. On October 12th, 1870, two men were taken off the Cardigan smack *Transit*, and on November 23rd, the lifeboat was launched to the aid of the *Chester*, which had been disabled in a storm and was in danger of being driven on to rocks at St David's Head. Coxswain David Hicks and his lifeboatmen brought the *Augusta* alongside the ship and helped to lay out her anchors. The *Chester*'s crew decided to return with the lifeboat and on the way back, the *Augusta* also took off the crews of the smacks *Anne Davies* and *Prima*. It was a fortunate move. That night,

the smacks dragged their anchors and fouled the *Chester*'s cables.

Many a good ship ended her days off St David's Head and in 1969, divers from the Swansea branch of the British Sub-Aqua Club located the wreck of a large sailing ship — believed to be the *Frederick* which was lost in 1833. She was trading between Britain and West Africa and finds from the wreck included clay pipes, beads, miniature bells, mugs and bowls, stoneware flagons, padlocks, brass rings, gunflints and iron spoons. Later dives by a Royal Navy team uncovered fancy razors, wrought iron bars and grapeshot, as well as an eight-foot long cannon. During the investigation of this wreck, a small wooden-hulled paddle steamer — thought to be the *Nimrod* — was also discovered.

Sledge Rocks, off the Head, claimed the brigantine *John Guise* on June 4th, 1850. This 111-ton ship was one of the first deep sea vessels built at Gloucester and during her 36-year career she carried cargoes to many ports throughout Europe. The steamship *Glenisla* had only been at sea for three years, when she was wrecked off St David's Head

Salvage operations underway on a small steamship – possibly the 'Emlyn', of Cardiff – at Llanpit, Fishguard Harbour.

(Picture: Studio Jon).

47

on the last day of February, 1886. The vessel was owned by Lindsay, Gracie and Company and was on passage from the Clyde with a cargo of coal for the Italian port of Savona on the Gulf of Genoa. The paddle steamer *Koh-i-Noor* was more fortunate. She was built on the Clyde at a cost of £50,000 and after trials set out for London. On May 28th, 1892, however, she ran onto rocks off St David's Head in dense fog. There was extensive damage to her bow section and, but for her watertight compartments, she would have sunk. The ship managed to limp as far as Milford Haven and, after repairs, she reached the Thames in the July to serve as a ferry between Clacton and Harwich.

On the south side of the Head — at Porthselau in Whitesands Bay — the paddle tug *Guiding Star* was wrecked in 1882. In April of the previous year, the 1,865-ton coaster *Amazon Ense* had been lost on the east side of the Head, at Porth-gwyn. The closing decade of the nineteenth century saw the tiny steamer *Musgrave* rendered a total loss on November 25th, 1892, on rocks near Pen Clegyr. She was on a voyage from Briton Ferry to Dundalk with coal. Nearby, at the tiny port of Porthgain, the British collier *Baron Ardrossan* was wrecked in August, 1898, while on her way from the Clyde to St Malo in France.

Fishguard was also having its share of disaster. The Norwegian barque *Evviva*, bound for Bristol with timber, drifted helplessly in mountainous seas in the bay on Saturday, November 18th, 1893. At one stage, it seemed as though she would strike the Cow and Calf rocks, but the storm then blew her to the far side of the bay towards Castle Point, under the old fort. Crowds of townspeople raced across the cliffs to the fort, only to see the barque veer off again and drift to the far side of the harbour. As they watched, a fifteen year old boy was washed overboard from the ship. Frantic crewmen threw him a line, which he grasped at the first attempt, but in the icy waters he lost his grip and was swept to his death.

When the *Evviva* finally struck the rocks, she went in stern first and each wave pushed her higher and higher on to the jagged shore, smashing her wooden hull wide open. Rescuers clambered along the rocks and

The Norwegian barque 'Evviva' aground on rocks in Fishguard Bay in November, 1893.   (Picture: Studio Jon).

successfully fired a line to the barque with the rocket apparatus. A seaman was brought ashore to begin with, but the line proved too thin and he received a severe buffetting. A thicker rope was passed to the ship and the captain's daughter was guided safely to land, to the cheers of the onlookers. The rest of the crew and the master, Captain H. Bauhn, were then brought off and were taken into Goodwick and Fishguard, where they were given dry clothing and lodgings.

On the Monday, the captain and his crew were able to return to the ship to retrieve their personal belongings, but there was no hope of saving the barque. She later broke up, sending her cargo and wreckage bobbing across the bay.

In the early hours of the same Saturday that the *Evviva* was wrecked, the Fishguard Lifeboat was launched to the aid of the collier *Warrenpoint*, of Newry. The ship had drifted on to Goodwick Sands in the storm. As the lifeboat was being launched in the darkness, the axle of its carriage broke and the reserve lifeboat had to be brought out. In the heavy seas, the lifeboat had difficulty in getting alongside the steamer, but

A trading schooner foundering off Goodwick Sands. The vessel may possibly be the 'Lizzie Edith', of Truro, which sank in a violent north-north-easterly gale in January, 1911. (Picture: Studio Jon).

eventually a rope was made fast and four men were taken off. The line parted before the remaining two survivors could jump on board and the lifeboat made a second run alongside to save them.

In another violent gale from the north-north-east in January, 1911, the Fishguard Lifeboat *Charterhouse* went to the aid of a number of vessels in distress — a familiar duty for this R.N.L.I. station.

Before dawn had broken on the second Thursday of that new year, the Hull steamship *Dynamo* lost both her anchors and was drifting towards the shore. Engine failure delayed the lifeboat and a Great Western Railway tug towed the *Charterhouse* out to the steamer, which was brought to safety with her crew of fourteen. The schooner *Lizzie Edith*, of Truro, had also dragged her anchors and was close to rocks when the lifeboat reached her. The crew was successfully taken off minutes before the schooner sank with her cargo of coal. By now, the lifeboat's engine was working again and she landed the crews of another schooner, *Agnes Craig*, the hopper dredger *Fishguard* and the ketch *Democrat*.

One of the last launches of the *Charterhouse*, with Lifeboat V.C. Coxswain Howells in command, was in 1922 under sails and motor. A three-masted Portuguese motor schooner, the *Lusitania 1*, was reported to be in a sinking condition about three miles north of Fishguard. But Coxswain Howells and his crew had no difficulty in picking her out, despite the darkness of that April night. The glare in the sky was brilliant. The schooner's crew had set fire to tar barrels to attract attention and she was now burning from stem to stern. She was in fact eighteen miles away — not three as was thought — and the lifeboat reached the wreck after a trying passage against a heavy head wind and sea, but there was no sign of life on board the ship, which was still burning furiously. A search was made of the area, without success, and it was later learned that the schooner's crew had been rescued by the steamer *Gaelic Star*. The wreck drifted to within eight miles of Fishguard before disappearing — and, the next morning, part of her cargo of pit props was found floating in the vicinity of Cemaes Head. When a Royal Navy destroyer patrolled the area looking for the wreck, which was a hazard to navigation, nothing was found, so the *Lusitania 1* was presumed to have sunk.

Fifty years later, the Fishguard Lifeboat *Howard Marryat* also put out to a ship on fire off the North Pembrokeshire coast. This vessel, too, became a hazard to shipping, but was successfully salvaged by the Milford Haven tug *Glengarth* and towed into port. The *Dolwen* — a former Milford Haven trawler — was returning from duties as a range safety vessel on the Royal Aircraft Establishment's missile range off Aberporth on December 18th, 1972, when fire broke out in her engine room. She was soon burning fiercely and the master, George Buchan and his crew of six were forced to take to a life-raft. They were picked up safely by the Fishguard Lifeboat. The fire wrecked the little craft but, after an extensive refit, she was able to return to her duties on the range within two years.

Another Milford trawler was not so fortunate and now slumbers on the sea bed less than a mile from Fishguard Harbour breakwater. The *William Rhodes Moorhouse*, an ex-Naval MFV, had left her home port for the Cardigan Bay fishing grounds on Easter Saturday, 1968. Her troubles began on Easter Monday afternoon — April 15th — after Skipper George Harding and his crew of five had made only eight or nine hauls. The trawler's winch developed a fault and they were assisted by the Swansea fishing vessel, *Lord Rodney*, which hauled up the gear.

That evening, the mate of the *William Rhodes Moorhouse*, George Paul, noticed the trawler was low in the water forward and the fish-room was found to be flooding. As their situation worsened, Skipper Harding made for the North Pembrokeshire coast and six miles off Strumble Head he sent out a 'Mayday' call. The six men launched the life-raft and were rescued by an oil tanker, the *Esso Purfleet*, which transferred them to the Fishguard Lifeboat. Later, after putting the skipper, mate and the boatswain, Billy Drake, back on board the trawler, the life-boat took the vessel in tow. As they were in sight of Fishguard Harbour the trawler began to list, and the lifeboat had to release the tow-line. The three men on board had seconds to get clear and, as they jumped into the sea, the *William Rhodes Moorhouse* went down. After being picked up and landed at Fishguard by the lifeboat, the survivors, who had only been in the water for a matter of minutes, were admitted to hospital suffering from shock and exposure.

The following year, the Fishguard Lifeboat *Howard Marryat* brought in ten survivors from the German motorship

The Fishguard Life-Boat 'Howard Marryat'.

(Picture: Western Telegraph).

Metric which sank in a 50 mph gale on December 14th. Captain Geisbert Volland, his wife and five year old son, the chief engineer and his wife, and five crew members, had been forced to abandon the ship off North Pembrokeshire when she developed a serious list. It proved impossible to launch the ship's boat and they had to scramble into a rubber raft as 18-foot high waves pounded the ship, which later rolled over and sank. The survivors were sighted by the Finnish cargo ship *Vega* and they were just being taken on board when the lifeboat arrived.

Coxswain Glyn Bateman took his boat alongside, but the conditions proved too dangerous to take the survivors off, so he decided to lead the *Vega* into the calmer waters of Fishguard Harbour. There, all were safely brought ashore. This lifeboat, the *Howard Marryat*, had replaced the *White Star*, which was based at Fishguard for 26 years from 1930. She was the gift to the R.N.L.I. of the Oceanic Steam Navigation Company — the White Star Line — and one of her last services was to the motor vessel *Gramsbergen* in 1954. This little Dutch

The Dutch coaster 'Gramsbergen' aground on rocks in Fishguard Bay in November, 1954. She later sank.
(Picture: Studio Jon).

coaster, completed only six months before, was forced onto rocks three minutes after her cable broke in a gale off Fishguard on November 27th. A 300-tonner, she was from Rotterdam's Furnace Line fleet, and had put into Fishguard Bay for shelter. Soon after she anchored, her skipper, J. L. Van Dullerman, was warned that his vessel was in the path of shipping — and he was asked to move her three lengths to port.

The manoeuvre was completed successfully in the darkness of that Saturday morning. But then the anchor chain parted and she was swept under cliffs between Dinas Head and Lower Fishguard. One of the crew, Pete Berkhuysen, volunteered to swim ashore with a lifeline and plunged into the freezing waters. Near the rocks, he was helped by farmer Jack Harries, who caught the lifeline and hauled him out of the sea. By this time, the Fishguard Lifeboat had reached the ship and taken off the captain and nine remaining crew members, as well as the *Gramsbergen's* mascots — two six-week old puppies! During the rescue operation, a rope fouled the lifeboat's propeller and the British Rail launch *Pencw*, which was

standing by, towed her back to the harbour to safely land the survivors. The *Pencw* was a former R.N.L.I. lifeboat which had saved two hundred and eighty two lives between 1923 and 1947. Optimistic that his ship could be towed off the rocks, when he was taken to the cliffs to see her, the *Gramsbergen's* captain was just in time to watch her slip slowly back into the sea. The little Dutch ship had been lost in a matter of hours.

Ironically, the ill-fated cattle freighter *El Tambo* lingered on for over two years. This 2,500 ton Panamanian vessel first hit the headlines in February, 1977, when she was towed into Fishguard Harbour after being crippled by fire while en route from Northern Ireland to Tripoli. Most of the crew were taken off by the British Rail ferry *Avalon*. Also involved in the rescue operation were the Royal Navy survey ship *H.M.S. Herald*, the Milford Haven tug *Exegarth*, the Naval salvage vessel *Garganey*, an oil rig supply ship, the *Arctic Seahorse* and the St David's Lifeboat. Fire was spreading through three decks and there was a high risk of explosion — but the blaze was fought

The cattle freighter 'El Tambo' under water at Fishguard Harbour in 1977.　　　(Picture: Western Telegraph).

bravely by naval fire fighters, led by Lieutenant Commander John Green and Petty Officer Peter Toms who were later both awarded Queen's Gallantry Medals.

When the *El Tambo* reached Fishguard Harbour, she was anchored less than a mile offshore. It was some days before the nine hundred cattle on board were transferred to

other ships — and then only after the personal intervention of the Prime Minister, James Callaghan. For six weeks, the vessel remained at her moorings as a legal wrangle began over salvage claims. Then, on Sunday, March 27th, 1977, she suddenly went down, bow first, and sank — her masts and part of her superstructure protruding sadly above the waves. A lone Italian seaman left on board was rescued by the Fishguard Lifeboat and transferred to an RAF Brawdy helicopter. A local salvage company, Diving International Engineering, won the contract to raise the ship, but was thwarted in its attempts. Although the vessel was brought to the surface at one stage, she tilted on her side and sank again. Early in 1979, it was revealed that the owners were abandoning the *El Tambo* and British Rail, as the harbour authority, was left with the task of seeking tenders for the removal of the wreck from the port.

The ill-fated freighter was finally removed from the harbour in June 1980 by a Southampton-based salvage firm, Risdon Beazley Marine. The wreck was cut into sections where she lay and transported by road to a scrapyard.

Wreck and Plunder

Shock waves of an explosion echoed around the cliffs of Druidston Haven and lifted a huge sand cloud over the scene as pebbles, hurled high into the air, ripped a horrific gap in the crowds who hurried down to the beach to join in the wrecking. One woman was already dead and the screams of the living mingled with the mournful cries of gulls disturbed by the blast as the gunpowder ignited. 'A providential judgment on the plunderers!' according to the local rector.

The Scarborough merchantman *Increase*, on charter to the British Ordnance Transport Service, had sailed from the West Indies in August, 1790, but it was a few days into January, 1791, before she was sighted off Pembrokeshire — and news quickly spread along the coast that there was a ship in trouble. The *Increase* was returning to England with a dangerous — if unattractive — cargo of condemned gunpowder from the British garrison on the Caribbean island of St Kitts. When she was driven ashore at Druidston, there were very few in the locality who were not aware of her plight — a situation which was to be exploited by those whose old habits died hard! The master of the *Increase*, Francis Pawson, the storekeeper Joseph Anthony, a woman passenger and the crew of eight, stayed with the ship until she was left high and dry on the sand by the receding tide. They then prepared to leave the vessel and a number of local people assisted them to unload their personal belongings. But as it was now dark, nothing further could be done until the next day. So the ship was left unprotected.

There were many more people than usual out and about the next morning. It was less than forty years since the reformed calendar was adopted and 'Old Christmas' — January 5th — was still observed as a Holy Day by many local people. A large crowd had gathered around the wreck of the *Increase* — some to plunder and others to help to unload the cargo into carts on the directions of the ship's master and the storekeeper. As the rum found on board began to flow, however, barrels of gunpowder were thrown over the side of the ship onto rocks, instead of to seaward. The plunderers had a particular fancy for the copper hoops around the barrels and soon the rocks were covered in gunpowder as the casks were smashed open. It was a situation ripe for disaster. And when a crowbar and a musket barrel were hurled over the side on to the rocks, sparks ignited the gunpowder. There were three devastating explosions. Over sixty people were burned. A young woman was killed on the spot and seven others were to linger for a few days before dying from their fearful injuries. Women fared worse than the men — as their flowing dresses burned fiercely; and almost everybody on the leeward side of the ship was scorched on face and hands. Many carried the marks of that day to their graves.

The Rector of Nolton Parish, the Rev. Moses Grant, left a vivid picture of the disaster in the parish records.

'The cliffs resounded with the groans of the miserable sufferers, with the lamentations and eager inquiries of fathers for their children, of husbands for their wives, of brothers for sisters, of children for their parents, everyone eventually being mutually anxious for the safety of his nearest relatives.

'This calamity,' he wrote, 'is plainly intended as a warning to desist from wreck plundering for none were hurt on the side next to the sea, where the persons stood who were endeavouring to save. This side only, where the explosion was, the plunderers stood. May this be a warning on future occasions, for it had but little effect on the spot . . . This memorandum is recorded by a spectator of the dismal scene, to perpetuate the memory of such a singular disaster, which points out a Providential judgement.'

Despite the catastrophe, plundering was to continue until late the next day, when a few militia men arrived — by which time, only the rigging and hull of the ship remained intact. Everything else had been stripped from the stranded vessel! A number of people were arrested by the militia but all who appeared for trial at Hereford a few months later were aquitted.

When Mary Morgan visited Pembrokeshire in August 1791, the wreck of the *Increase* was still on the beach. In her book, *A Tour of Milford Haven*, she reveals that she and a companion tied their horse and chaise to the bowsprit of the ship. She refers to the plunderers as 'of the very lowest order of the community'.

'Would I could with truth add that this melancholy catastrophe has produced a thorough change in the conduct of the inhabitants of this rocky coast. But, I fear, they do not yet feel all that sympathy for the distresses of shipwrecked mariners, which naturally arises in the breasts of those, who are less habituated to such scenes of woe. Indeed, there is too much reason to believe, that they experience nearly the same sensations at the sight of a ship labouring in a storm, as arises in the mind of an undertaker, when he contemplates the declining health of a wealthy citizen.'

It appears, though, that a lesson *was* learned from the *Increase* disaster. On Christmas Day, 1810, another ship was wrecked at Druidston Haven — the *Linen Hall*, of Dublin, bound to the West Indies in ballast. Very little was plundered from the vessel, which was eventually broken up and the timber and rigging was **SOLD** to the local people!

The timber barque 'Dorchester' on Tenby's North Sands, where she was beached and broken up in 1829, after stranding near Ragwen Point, Pendine.
(From a Charles Norris watercolour in the Tenby Museum collection).

Gunpowder was carried on board the *Loch Shiel* — wrecked near the South Pembrokeshire village of Angle in 1894 — but it was her whisky which contributed to the deaths of three men. The story of the *Loch Shiel* has become part of the county's folk lore and has overshadowed what was a brilliant rescue operation by Angle lifeboatmen. The full-rigged iron ship was on a voyage from her home port of Glasgow to Adelaide and Melbourne on the night of Tuesday, January 30th, when she stranded in heavy seas on Thorn Island at the entrance to Milford Haven. Captain Thomas Davies, master of the *Loch Shiel*, tried the pump and found a quantity of water. The ship was, in fact, sinking rapidly by the stern and he ordered the boats out. A mattress soaked with paraffin was burnt as a distress signal and the St Ann's Head Coastguard telegraphed Angle with the news that a ship was in trouble.

It was 10.45 p.m. when the Angle Lifeboat, *Henry Martin Harvey*, set out for Thorn Island — less than two miles away. As the lifeboat neared the *Loch Shiel*, the anchor was dropped and the boat's bow was brought to the mizzen rigging. Six men were brought to safety from the mizzen top, although there was considerable difficulty in getting one of them, an invalid passenger, on board. The lifeboat now pulled to the lee side of the island to take off the remainder of the passengers and crew, who had clambered along the jib-boom on to rocks. Lifeboat honorary secretary, R. W. Mirehouse, who had accompanied the boat, and lifeboatmen Edward Ball and Thomas Rees, landed on the island and with a rope and lantern crawled along the edge of the cliff. It was pitch dark and in some places, the path was less than a foot wide. They reached the spot, below which the *Loch Shiel*'s passengers and crew had taken refuge, and lowered the rope down the cliff. All twenty-seven survivors on the rocks, including a woman passenger who was very weak and exhausted, were hauled to safety. But the party still had to negotiate the treacherous clifftop path in the darkness.

The return journey was extremely difficult, Mr Mirehouse and the two lifeboatmen having to guide the passengers and crew every step of the way back to the

This Charles Norris painting of an unknown shipwreck – possibly the collier brig 'Durham' wrecked at Saundersfoot in February 1839 – shows some of the crew clinging to life in the fore top. (From the Norris collection at Tenby Museum).

lifeboat. Twenty of the survivors were taken on board the lifeboat, which landed them at Angle and then returned for the others. By 6.30 a.m. on the Wednesday, all seven passengers and twenty-six crew members from the *Loch Shiel* were on the mainland. Some were cared for at Mr Mirehouse's home at Angle Hall and others were given shelter in the village. As daylight dawned, the tide brought in wreckage and cargo, including a large consignment of whisky. Customs officers swooped onto the beach and recovered sixty cases, but much more had already been 'spirited' away! The whisky — all 100° proof — was hidden in roofs, holes in the cliffs and buried in the vicinity. Indeed, it was so well hidden in some instances that it remained concealed for years. In the 1950s two bottles of *Loch Shiel* whisky were found during repair work on the roof of an Angle home.

Mrs Lily Rees — who died a few years ago in her nineties — was only ten when the *Loch Shiel* was wrecked. She remembered carrying home from the beach what she thought was a keg of butter. In fact it was gunpowder, which was used for many years to fire a salute every time there was a wedding in the village. Much of the *Loch Shiel*'s general cargo went into storage at Milford Haven, but for several days after the wreck, cases of whisky were being washed up along the shores of the Haven. For one young man, the whisky proved deadly. He and his brother found a case of the spirits on a beach a few miles west of Milford, partook freely and quickly became very drunk. They managed to stagger up from the shore, but then one of them collapsed unconscious at the roadside. His brother groped his way home and made no attempt to return when he had sobered up. But as the missing brother often slept out, the family were not alarmed when he failed to return home. Two days later, his body was found in a hedge and at the inquest the cause of his death was given as 'excessive whisky drinking'. The Coroner heard evidence that when the *Loch Shiel* was wrecked, between fifty and a hundred people were on the beach, drinking and carrying away whisky.

A father and son were drowned that same week, attempting to tow a keg ashore from the wreck. Their boat capsized in the rough seas and both were swept away to their deaths. A second son managed to cling to the keel of the upturned boat and was saved.

The *Loch Shiel* affair switched to Glasgow late in February, 1894, when Captain Thomas Davies appeared before a Board of Trade inquiry. Sheriff Guthrie, who presided, said the court found that proper measures were not taken to ascertain the position of the ship. The master alone was in default. He had been on deck all the time and was in sole charge of navigation. Captain Davies was an officer who had an extremely good record, said Sheriff Guthrie. His character was of the best and this was the first time, as far as they knew, that he had been in any trouble of that kind. However, the court felt it had no alternative but to suspend his Master's certificate for three months, but he was granted a Mate's ticket.

The Angle Lifeboat heroes were honoured for their bravery by the R.N.L.I., which voted silver medals to Mr Mirehouse, Thomas Rees and Edward Ball in recognition of 'the intrepidity displayed by them on this occasion'. The *Loch Shiel*'s owners, the Glasgow Shipping Company, added their thanks to the lifeboat and the master, Thomas Davies, wrote praising Mr and Mrs Mirehouse and all the villagers for their hospitality and kindness. The *Loch Shiel* became a total wreck, but her name lives on in the legend of whisky galore!

When later in 1894 the Spanish steamer *Tormes* was wrecked off Linney Head, it was clear that the authorities were determined to avoid a repetition of the *Loch Shiel* plundering. The Coastguard and Police launched patrols of the cliffs and beaches — although it was fruit, and not whisky, which this time came floating in on the breakers. The *Tormes* was on passage from Malaga to Liverpool, with a cargo of Spanish fruit and vegetables, when she struck. Of her crew of twenty-eight, only seven survived and they were picked up by the trawler *Exmouth* and landed at Milford. The *Tormes* was wrecked on the night of October 30th and the next day, the sands at Freshwater West were strewn with boxes of oranges, lemons, almonds, raisins and onions. The air stank with the smell of the onions and the ship's cargo was strewn over two miles along the shore. Hundreds of people flocked to the sands, which were well guarded, but found that much of the fruit was not worth salvaging. For the *Tormes*, it was a sad end to her first voyage under the Spanish flag. She broke in two — another victim of Linney Head's notorious Crow Rock. She was not the first ship from Malaga to founder on the Pembrokeshire coast, however. On Christmas Eve, 1668, John Powell, writing from Milford to James Hickes in London, reported that the *Amity*, of Southampton, had been 'cast away near St David's Head' on December 16th. The ship was carrying wine and fruit from Malaga when she was hit by a violent storm while at anchor in Ramsey Sound and driven ashore. 'Nothing to be supposed but death, the men deserted her and went ashore on Ramsey Island,' wrote Powell. 'The ship ran ashore near St David's Head, where the country people were so barbarous that they staved the wine casks in so much that the master saved not anything considerable, only some fruit which we indemnified. The officers of the Customs were there and could not find out one cask of wine.'

Wines and spirits were particular favourites of the 'beachcombers', but some coastal folk were unlucky enough to be caught in the act. A North Pembrokeshire man was arrested by Customs officers while carrying away a keg of brandy from a wreck, and he was sentenced to hard labour in a Portsmouth prison. Occasionally, there was a chance for the women to pick up valuable rolls of cloth. To avoid detection as they made for home, the women would wind the cloth around the waists and under their skirts. There was also the judgment of fate for some wrongdoers. A pregnant woman who stripped the clothes off the body of a baby washed ashore from a Solva wreck, was said to have died with her own baby at the confinement. It happened at the wreck of the *Phoebe and Peggy*, which went down near the entrance to Solva Harbour in January, 1773. Over sixty people drowned, including the baby and a Lady, whose fingers were broken by plunderers stealing her gold rings. The woman's nephew survived the wreck but was only able to recover a few of his aunt's possessions. A number of Solva men put out in boats in a brave rescue operation, but on the return trip one of the craft was swamped and all on board were lost. A ballad was written in memory of those who died. Here is part of it, as published in Eric Freeman's 'The Solva Saga':

A ship was built in Philadelphia,
The capital of Pennsylvania.
When she bore out all for the channel,
New Christmas Day she took her farewell.
With merry hearts they sailed for Newry.
First land they speid was the isle of Ramsey.
They set their compass to the North-west,
The hurricane came from the South-west.
Into Bride's Bay she was well recorded.
Where many a thousand souls were drowned.
The night came on, she met the races,
She struck a rock down near St Elvis,
Four lusty men came out from Solva,
And eighteen more from Philadelphia,
One was single, three was married,
The boat turned round and they were drowned.
There was some wives, there was some children,
Aboard the ship their cry was dismal;
The weakest sort was left to drowndy,
I hope the Lord have showed them mercy.
Madam Elliott she was drowned,
Five hundred guineas in her pocket.
And old Luke Davy and John Phillip

They robbed the lady in a minute.
And for her rings they cut her fingers,
And split her ears all for her jewels.
These country mobs they be like villains,
They stripped the ladies of their jewels.
After they had robbed the ladies,
They left them there like stinking fishes,
Till gentlemen came bury the ladies,
In Brawdy Church down near St Elvis,
When you rises in the morning,
Pray to God to give his blessing —
Nobody knows at sunrising
What may happen before the evening.

Eighty-nine years later, when the *Oak*, of Belfast, was wrecked off Solva, the seamen who survived had their clothes stolen by local rogues. James Nash, whose notebooks provide an insight into some of the shipwrecks in the area, recorded that he later had to tour the village to obtain garments for the survivors. The *Oak* was wrecked on the morning of October 17th, 1862, and six seamen took refuge on a rock. They were eventually brought ashore after a lifeline had been fired to them by means of Manby mortar life-saving apparatus.

'All the men and a boy were brought to safety,' wrote Nash. 'The boy was the last but one coming ashore in the breeches buoy and the last man had the easiest transit to the shore through the breakers and stones as if to recompense him for his great care of the boy.'

The survivors were taken to the village's Cambrian Hotel by the local Lloyd's agent, Captain John Rees, and Nash went around Solva in search of clothes.

'Having clothed the boy with a suit of my own clothes, I had courage to ask the others to give and glad am I to say they had plenty of clothes to give them, such as stockings, flannels, shirts, trousers, vests, also some money for each to have in his pocket.'

One of the many legends relating to South Pembrokeshire's St Govan's Chapel — tucked away beneath wild and towering cliffs — centres on the theft of a silver bell by pirates. The story goes that before the pirate's ship was out of sight of the chapel 'a storm instantly sprang up and the sacrilege was punished by the vessel being wrecked'.

Bells stolen in the 17th century from St Justinian's Chapel, near St David's, are said to have been lost in a wreck in Ramsey Sound and 'now chime only during great gales'. Some ships were lured on to rocks by false lights from the shore. But for a member of one South Wales family, such practices ended in personal tragedy. He was making plans to plunder one wreck, when the body of his own son was washed ashore from the ship. Overcome with remorse, he moved away from the area and died later at Tenby, where he lived in seclusion.

Deadly Doctrine

It was a miracle that anyone survived. For two nights and a day, they clung to the masts of the stricken ship swept by tempestuous seas. Hour after hour the wind shrieked and tore at their clothes, its icy hand numbing their hungry bodies. Yet still they hung on to life — their plight hidden from shore by the wintry shroud of a January storm. When daylight broke after the second night, the seven were near to death. But help was within sight — the brave little lifeboat *Gem* thrusting towards them, her crew straining at the oars in the tide rip of Ramsey Sound. For one of the seamen, however, it was already too late. He was still lashed to the rigging of the wreck, but the ordeal had finally taken its toll and only six men were brought off alive by the St David's Lifeboat.

When the survivors reached the shelter of the mainland, the full story of their agony was slowly unfolded. Their ship, the Grimsby steamer *Graffoe* had left Glasgow on January 23rd, 1903, bound for Montevideo. She ran into a storm in the Irish Sea, strayed from her course and in the darkness of January 25th, she ran on to the southern end of Ramsey Island. Fourteen men got into one of the ship's lifeboats and were ordered to stand by under the lee of the vessel. But heavy seas swept the boat away and it was late in the afternoon of the 26th when these survivors were picked up 30 miles away by a steamer and landed at Penarth. The conditions prevented a second ship's boat being launched so the rest of the crew sought safety on the bridge and in the rigging. When the ship settled down in the sea soon afterwards, the master and chief engineer were washed overboard and were drowned. Only seven men now remained on board.

The storm continued until 10 a.m. on the 27th, when the wreck was sighted from the shore. The St David's Lifeboat was launched and ran a great risk in approaching the ship because of the strong wind, the set of the tide and current, and the proximity of dangerous rocks. When a line was secured to the *Graffoe*, the dead man was the first to be brought off. The lifeboat's acting coxswain, William Narbett — who was to die later that same year — was awarded the R.N.L.I.'s silver medal for this gallant and meritorious service. Each of the crew was given a special monetary reward.

Ramsey is a magical emerald of an island set a mile off the St David's Peninsula in wicked seas, which bear no mercy to the mariner in distress. The two-masted Chepstow sailing coaster, *Warren*, homeward bound from Dublin was lost in Ramsey Sound on December 19th, 1815, fortunately without loss of life. One of the services of the first St David's Lifeboat, the *Augusta*, was to a brigantine which had stranded on the island on November 11th, 1877. A west-south-westerly gale, with heavy rain, prevented the lifeboat being launched until early the following morning. When she did hit the waters of the Sound, her crew had to pull hard for four hours to reach the ship — the *Mystic Tie*, of Ardrossan.

The ship's mate and six crew members had climbed on to a rock and had to be hauled through the surf to the *Augusta* in a life-buoy. The last man to leave the rock was knocked over by a giant breaker and his life-

Captain David Hicks, coxswain of the first St. David's Life-Boat 'Augusta', which was in service from 1869-1885. The boat was ten-oared and saved 23 lives.

(Picture: R.N.L.I.).

line twisted around his wrist and foot. Coxswain David Hicks urged his crew forward and, as they bent to the oars, the lifeboat pushed in amongst the white waters. The bowman cut the line and others seized the sinking survivor as the lifeboat shot back out to safety.

It was later learned that the master of the *Mystic Tie* and one crew member had managed to swim ashore, but another seaman was drowned. For this rescue, Coxswain Hicks and the bowman, Captain John Rees, the honorary lifeboat secretary, were voted the R.N.L.I.'s Thanks inscribed on Vellum. The crew received an extra monetary award. David Hicks served as coxswain for twenty-three years and was presented with the Institution's long service medal. The lifeboat *Augusta* accompanied him into retirement. When she was due to be replaced, he bought her for use as a chicken coop on his farm!

At the end of 1903 — which had opened with the loss of the *Graffoe* — the iron steamship *Count D'Aspremont* foundered in Ramsey Sound after running on to the Horse Rock. She was on passage from Dublin to Newport and went down on December 15th. Ivor Arnold, who served as coxswain of the St David's Lifeboat for five years from 1913, and 13 years from 1923, was farming Ramsey when an Austrian steamer, the *Szent Istvan*, sank south-west of the island in 1908. A 7,000 tonner, en route from Oporto to Glasgow with a general cargo, she hit rocks in dense fog on September 28th. The captain and crew of twenty-six reached the island in the ship's boat and were given food and tea by Ivor Arnold. Later, he piloted them to the mainland.

West of Ramsey is the South Bishop Lighthouse, perched high on an islet, which forms part of a three mile chain of rocks — the Bishops and Clerks — which were described by the Elizabethan antiquary George Owen as preaching 'deadly doctrine to their winter audience'. But they held no terror for Mrs Thomas Williams, of Treleddyn, near St David's. It was in 1780, or thereabouts, when through her telescope she picked out the crew of a Swedish ship which had been wrecked on the Bishops. She launched a boat to go to their aid. One of the seamen was swept away, but seven took refuge on one of the rocks and were all rescued by Mrs Williams — Pembrokeshire's own Grace Darling.

In 1855, Army recruits travelling on the packet steamer *Morna* were of a less hardy breed. They had joined the little ship at Belfast late on Saturday, February 24th. But nineteen hours out, on passage to London, the ship struck the North Bishop. Strong cross currents in the Irish Sea had pushed the ship well off course in dense fog — so thick that at times the master, Captain Carter, could not even see as far as the bow. The *Morna* struck at about seven on the Sunday evening and although her engines were put astern, she failed to come off the rocks. As a result, there was a general rush for the boats. Captain Carter attempted to calm the passengers, most of whom were Army recruits, and urged them not to panic. The port boat and quarter boat were successfully lowered and got clear of the wreck with a number of passengers and crew. Several of the remaining recruits then rushed for the jolly boat and, launched in haste, the craft was swamped and most of those in the boat were drowned.

The steamer was being dashed by heavy seas, which stove in a fourth boat on the deck. When the *Morna* began to break up, the remaining passengers and members of the crew were stranded on the after part of the ship, as the cargo of beef, pork, whiskey and Irish linen floated around them. Eventually, the starboard lifeboat was launched and all were taken off, Captain Carter being the last to leave the wreck. The boat reached Ramsey at five the following morning and later they made their way to the mainland. The other survivors from the *Morna* were picked up by a passing ship and landed at Milford Haven. Of the ninety-three people on board the little packet steamer when she sailed from Belfast, twenty-one Army recruits and seamen were lost in the disaster.

When the Liverpool schooner *Mersey* sank off the South Bishop on June 5th, 1872, the lighthouse keepers sent up signals of distress. These were answered by the St David's Lifeboat *Augusta* and the schooner's crew of four were all rescued.

The *Augusta* was replaced in 1885 by the *Gem*, which in May, 1904, brought the crew of five of the barque *Edith Crossfield* to safety. The vessel went aground on the North Bishop in thick fog, on her way from Lancashire to London, and the crew clambered on to the rocks where they huddled for over 40 hours, surviving on biscuits and water, until sighted by a passing steamer.

Two years later — in November, 1906 — the Cardiff collier *Ross* was wrecked on the Bishops. The crew took to the boats and were rescued by the Bristol-Dublin steamer *Argo*. One of the largest ships to succumb to the 'deadly doctrine' of the Bishops was the 5,852 ton cargo steamer *Langton Grange*. She stranded on the North Bishop on August 5th, 1909, on a voyage from the Clyde to South Wales, in ballast, and fog was again partly to blame for the incident. Although the ship's signals of distress were heard on the mainland, her exact position was not known. As a result, St David's Lifeboat, the *Gem*, made a somewhat protracted search before the casualty was found. Coxswain John Stephens, who was to be lost in the *Gem* disaster the following year, took the lifeboat alongside the ship in difficult conditions and boarded the vessel. The master of the *Langton Grange*, Captain Groves, asked the lifeboat to stand by, but after three hours he decided that the entire crew would remain on board as there were other ships in the vicinity. The lifeboat returned to her station, which she had left eight tiring hours earlier. Later, the *Langton Grange* was abandoned and Captain Groves and his crew of 53 were taken off by a steamer.

Nearly seven miles south of Ramsey is Skomer Island, which is seperated from its northern cousin by the eastward sweep of St Bride's Bay 'within which there is safe riding for ships with all winds between south and north-east', as the British Channel Pilot of 1859 warned: 'with the wind to the southward and westward, and when blowing strong, a heavy sea sets into the bay, which might make it difficult, particularly for deeply-laden vessels, to work out. Care should be taken, therefore, not to be caught there'. A great many ships *were* caught there, despite the warnings, and paid the price. The schooner *Sarah*, of Strangford in Northern Ireland, was wrecked on October

22nd, 1873, during a moderate gale from the north-west to west. Her crew of four were saved by the Solva Lifeboat, *Charles and Margaret Egerton*, which was on service for 11 hours in darkness. This was the only occasion on which lives were saved by the Solva boat. She was launched on service only four times during the 18-year history of the station, which was opened in 1869 and closed in 1887. The lifeboat was sold and returned to sea as a fishing craft.

It had been found impossible to launch the lifeboat from Solva at low tide and in certain storm conditions she was unable to pass the Black Rock at the entrance to the little port. This meant that the St David's Lifeboat reached ships in distress earlier than the Solva boat. Some twenty-three years before the arrival of the lifeboat at Solva, the Irish schooner *Victoria*, of Youghal, was driven on to rocks close to the harbour entrance in a November gale. One survivor reached the shore, only to be swept off his feet by the huge waves. In his struggle for life, his shirt became entangled around his head and when he next came ashore he was already dead. A woman passenger clung desperately to a boom, but as her grip finally failed, she was washed away. Six men from the ship managed to climb onto a rock and cried out for help, but because of the conditions no boat could reach them. When darkness fell, they were still on the rock. By daylight, they had all disappeared. Had they remained on board the wreck, they would have been saved, for the vessel slipped off the rocks and drifted high and dry on to the beach.

In 1874, the Liverpool ship *Alaric* foundered in St Bride's Bay. She was sighted, bottom up, a mile west of the Green Scar Rock, off Solva, and later sank with the loss of all hands.

One of the great mysteries of St Bride's Bay centres on the origin of a giant anchor, which now rests two miles inland at Anchor Hoaten, between St Bride's and St Ishmaels. The anchor is over 17 feet long and nearly 13 feet wide at the flukes and is believed to have been recovered from a wreck close inshore. It was then abandoned at the roadside during its journey inland and was hauled to its present site on two pairs of cart wheels in the early 1890s. The identity of the ship on which it was carried, however, remains unknown.

In 1971, divers from the Cardiff-based Dolphin Sub-Aqua Club found five 19th century naval cannons in the bay. A sub-aqua survey a few years earlier also located the wreck of the little wooden auxiliary vessel *Portland*, which sank on December 9th, 1927, carrying stone from Porthgain to Pembroke. In the same area, off Porthlysgi Bay, divers found the remains of the steamship *Whiteplain*, and about five miles south-west by west, a Royal Navy survey ship pinpointed the wreck of the Dutch motorship *Wiema*, which went down in December, 1961, when her cargo shifted in a heavy gale. A century before, the Cardigan sloop *Surprise* sank in St Bride's Bay when she was run down by the Dublin schooner *Isabella*. The crew just had time to get on board the

The giant anchor from a mystery wreck in St. Bride's Bay. The anchor now rests two miles inland at Anchor Hoaten, near St. Ishmaels, and is over 17 feet long and nearly 13 feet wide at the flukes. (Picture: Martin Cavaney).

schooner before the sloop went down — on April 5th, 1860. The *Request*, of Swansea, had also been lost that Spring, with her cargo of tar.

Villagers at Newgale — one of the coastal communities on St Bride's Bay — awoke a few days before Christmas, 1974, to find the motor yacht *Attacker* stranded on the beach after a force nine gale. She was on charter to the Ministry of Defence for duties on the Royal Aircraft Establishment's missile range in Cardigan Bay, when fire broke out in her engine room. Taken in tow from Fishguard to Milford Haven by the tug *Bristolian*, the line parted in the storm and the unmanned *Attacker* later drifted ashore, badly holed.

The paddle steamer *Albion* was the pride of the Cork to Bristol service. She was famed for her fast passages across the Irish Sea and travellers enjoyed a fine programme of entertainment on the journey from a resident band. In 1833, two years after she was launched, she was said to have completed a 700 mile double sailing — Waterford — Bristol — Cork — Bristol — in 70 hours. Her quest for speed took her on

The motor yacht 'Attacker' aground on Newgale Beach in December, 1974. (Picture: Western Telegraph).

a voyage to disaster in April, 1837, when she hit a submerged rock while taking a short cut through the notorious Jack Sound. The paddler was run on to sands near Marloes and her fifty passengers and crew were saved, as well as five horses and one hundred and eighty pigs. After most of her moveable equipment had been salvaged, however, she broke up on the beach which now bears her name — Albion Sands. Two iron shafts protruding from the shore at low tide are now the last memorial to this little ship.

Sands at Marloes were also the last resting place of the wooden paddler, *Lass of Gowrie*, which foundered there on October 26th,

1881. Jack Sound, where spring tides run through at five to six knots, claimed the 500-ton steamship *Lonsdale* on an October Sunday in 1938. A Swansea coaster, she was returning, light, from Ireland when she ran short of fuel after battling against an autumn gale. She anchored off Martins Haven and took on enough coal to take her to Milford Haven. She took the short cut through the Sound, but hit the Crab Stones rock and was swept on to Midland Island, where nine years before the *Molesey* had struck. The crew were ordered to take to the ship's boat by the master, Skipper J. Hegarty, but he refused to leave the dying *Lonsdale*. Reuben Codd, who was farming Skomer Island, put out from Martins Haven in his motor boat with his wife, Betty, and her father, Walter Sturt, and towed the crew's boat clear of Jack Sound. He then returned to the *Lonsdale* and finally persuaded Skipper Hegarty to leave the ship. The Angle Lifeboat was launched, but returned to her station when it became clear that the master and crew had been saved.

A 450 ton Dutch coaster sparked off a

The 450 ton Dutch coaster 'Lucy' with her stern aground on the Blackstones rock in Jack Sound on February 14th, 1967. Her skipper and crew were rescued from a life-raft, but the ship later drifted clear of the rock and sank. (Picture: Royal Navy).

major alert in the Sound in 1967, when she grounded with her stern on the Blackstones rock. The ship was en route from Norway to Barry with a cargo of calcium carbide, which it was feared would explode should it come into contact with water. She struck the rock at about noon on February 14th and within thirty minutes, her skipper, Jan Spaltman and his crew, had got clear on a life-raft. They were picked up safely, together with the mascot of the Dutch ship, a collie dog. The vessel — named *Lucy* — disappeared in a snow storm and was last seen with her decks awash in St Bride's Bay.

In January, 1882, the Holme Line steamer *Thomas Vaughan* went missing off the Pembrokeshire coast, with the loss of all hands, and it was later discovered that she had foundered in the Sound. A valuable cargo of salt, on its way to Haverfordwest, was lost off Skomer during the 18th century when the *Mayflower* was wrecked. One of the most famous of the two-masted trading schooners of the 1920s was the *Alice Williams*, built at Llanelli back in 1854. But her sailing days ended in February, 1928, when she ran ashore, with all her sails set, in a cove on the bird sanctuary island of Skokholm. The ship had been abandoned, leaking, off Milford Haven, but when she drifted on to the island it proved a godsend for naturalist Ronald Lockley who was farming Skokholm. He bought the wreck for £5 and salvaged her cargo of coal and many of her fittings, some of which are still on the island. The schooner's figurehead was carried to a rock, above the cove where she came ashore, and there she keeps a lonely vigil.

Less than six years after the packet steamer *Albion* was run ashore near Marloes, another Bristol packet steamer, the *Queen*, was lost on Skokholm. She was on the outward run to Dublin late on Friday, September 1st, 1843, when she ran aground in thick fog. One of her passengers was drowned in his berth, but the other twenty and the sixteen crew members were rescued by the Milford sloop, *Hope*.

Between Skomer and the Smalls is the lonely island of Grassholm, which provided the Angle Lifeboat, *Henry Martin Harvey*, with one of her most difficult rescues. The schooner *Ellen* was running for the shelter of

The Llanelli-built schooner 'Alice Williams', wrecked on Skokholm Island in February, 1928.

(Picture: National Maritime Museum).

Milford Haven on December 8th, 1893, when she lost her sails and was driven ashore on the island. Five of her crew scrambled off the ship and they later found their skipper lying unconscious on rocks. A shelter was built for him, but when they were rescued by a boat from the Milford trawler *Birda* twenty-four hours later, it proved impossible to move the injured skipper across the rocks. He was left on the island, and the Angle Lifeboat was alerted to go to his aid. She was towed out to Grassholm by another Milford trawler, *Her Majesty*, but darkness and the terrible breakers around the island prevented a landing being made. The vessels had to return to the Haven and retraced their course when the weather had moderated, by which time the skipper, who unfortunately was without food or water, was already dead.

The rocks around the Smalls are among the most treacherous on the British coastline and have claimed hundreds of lives from wrecks. The building of successive lighthouses there was an epic effort in itself and when the light was extinguished during an October storm in 1812, a number of ships

Lonely Grassholm Island, where the skipper of the wrecked schooner 'Ellen' died in December, 1893. The ex-German steamer 'Walter L. M. Russ' was wrecked on the island's rocks in July, 1945. (Picture: Martin Cavaney).

foundered. One of these was the brig *Fortitude*, which went down with her crew of eleven in the December. Even when the light was operational, wrecks still occurred with regularity, if not in such large numbers. As recently as 1967, the coaster *Luminence* was lost off the Smalls and in 1978 the giant oil tanker, *Christos Bitas*, grounded on the neighbouring Hats and Barrels reef — an incident which resulted in her eventually being scuttled far out into the Atlantic.

The coaster 'Luminence' listing heavily after running on to the Smalls in March, 1967. She sank soon afterwards.

(Picture: R.N.A.S. Brawdy).

The *Luminence* struck the Smalls shortly after three on a Wednesday afternoon, March 1st, and was badly holed. Her crew took to a raft and were saved in a brilliant rescue operation by a helicopter from the Royal Naval Air Station at Brawdy. The Navy pilot, Lieutenant Derek Scott, brought the helicopter in over the life-raft with great skill and daring and the survivors were winched, one by one, to safety. The helicopter then transferred them to the British ship, *Patroclus*, which had to lower one of her masts to enable the helicopter to get close enough. The transfer was completed successfully as the *Patroclus* pitched and rolled in the heavy seas. As the crew reached the deck, they were just in time to see the *Luminence* go down.

Skill and daring also saved the crew of the steamer *George Moore*, which hit the Smalls on May 20th, 1887, in a severe gale. Her distress signals were sighted by the Bristol-Cork paddler *Juno* and her captain, L. G. Starr, took his ship as close as he dared to the jagged rocks. A boat was launched by the *Juno*'s mate, Tom Eastaway, and a number of the crew, and in two trips they took off all

sixteen survivors from the sinking *George Moore*. For this rescue, Captain Starr and Tom Eastaway received silver medals for bravery from the R.N.L.I.

Three years before, only seven of the crew of the Cory cargo ship, *Rhiwabon*, survived when she was wrecked on those rocks on January 29th, 1884. The ship was on a voyage, in ballast, from Fleetwood to Cardiff and the survivors were picked up by the Bristol-Wexford steamer, *Briton*. Hardly a year passed without a wreck on the Smalls and the roll of disaster seems endless: the tug *Gulliver* in June, 1887; the Bombay-bound cargo ship *Drumburlie* in April, 1891; the ore carrier *Rowena* in May, 1893; the Milford trawler *Tantallon Castle* in January, 1908, and the *Cambro* in May, 1913.

In July, 1897, the paddle steamer *Hibernia* was on her way to a Bristol breakers yard, when she parted her tow from the tug *Kestrel* in a heavy westerly gale. She was abandoned close to the Smalls and the five crew members on board the old steamer were hauled to the *Kestrel* by line. Even 'ghost ships' were sighted in the vicinity of the Smalls. The ketch *Meridian* was on passage from the Cornish port of Par to Runcorn in 1921, when she grounded in thick fog. She was abandoned by her crew, who stood by the ketch for 17 hours. When they lost sight of her, it was presumed she had sunk and her crew were rescued by a trawler and taken to Milford Haven. In fact, the *Meridian* had refloated and passed her crew sailing unmanned for nearly 100 miles before going ashore on the Irish coast. Another 'ghost ship' was the *Sarah Macdonald*, which struck the Smalls on October 7th, 1911. The St David's Lifeboat saved the captain and crew, who had taken refuge on rocks. But their ship slipped off the reef and sailed off, with the lifeboat in pursuit. The deserted ship was eventually overhauled, but when her master inspected the damage, he realised she could not be saved and she was left to sink.

One of the worst shipwrecks on the Hats and Barrels reef occurred in 1892, when the four-masted ship *Earl of Aberdeen* was lost. The 2,205 ton vessel, owned by the Earl Sailing Ship Line, struck the rocks on the afternoon of May 15th. She was on a voyage from Barry to Montevideo with coal. Two of her crew managed to get away in a boat, but the others sought the safety of the rigging as the ship sank under them. The steamship *Mary Hough* sent a rescue boat, but it was unable to reach the wreck because of the heavy swell. The Royal Navy gunboat, *H.M.S. Foxhound*, took off several men, but the survivors in the fore rigging would not attempt to work aft to safety and were drowned. Eleven of the crew and five apprentices were lost, and the captain and first officer were among those who were saved. The same reef was at the centre of the mystery disappearance of the Spanish cargo ship, *Mar Del Plata*. She left the Clyde on January 30th, 1923, with coal for Bilbao, but was never heard of again and her wreck is believed to lie off these quaintly-named, but lethal, rocks.

Voyage to Disaster

The carnage that was the *Mars* was bloody and terrible. The rocks and sand at Freshwater West were strewn with the dead, and each tide brought a fresh wave of horror. Amidst the carcasses of livestock, the bodies of men, women and children were hurled ashore by the Atlantic breakers. Coastal folk wept as they counted the cost of that cruel sea. Horrific were the scenes around the dying ship as she sank off the South Pembrokeshire coast. Passengers and crew struggled for life with pigs, horses and cattle whose horns were no less deadly than the jagged rocks under Linney Head.

When daylight dawned, there were just six survivors.

The voyage to disaster had begun at the Irish port of Waterford on a Tuesday morning, April 1st, in 1862. The packet steamer *Mars* had already been in service with the Waterford and Bristol Steam Navigation Company for 13 years. But she was a sturdy iron vessel and was a fine sight under steam and full sail as she headed out into the Irish Sea for the West Country. Captain Blynman and his twenty-three officers and men had welcomed some thirty passengers on board for the voyage. Eleven had been booked into cabins, including a retired captain of the East India Company, a mother and child, and a businessman's daughter described as 'a very amiable and interesting young lady'. The ship's cargo included about 180 head of horned cattle; 137 pigs and 10 horses, as well as boxes of eggs, fish and poultry. A number of cattle dealers had missed the sailing at Waterford's Quay, but had cut across country in a carriage and had boarded the ship in the Passage. The crossing to the Welsh coast was uneventful and even when the *Mars* ran into fog as darkness fell, there was no hint of the danger into which she was sailing. But as she began moving up the Bristol Channel she was already off course — a fact of which no-one on board was aware. For, when she struck the rocks off Linney Head, she was under full steam with all her sails set. The speed at which she ran aground ripped her wide open, yet she might have remained afloat for some time. However, when

Captain Blynman ordered her engines to be put astern, her single screw bit into the sea and hauled her off the rocks. Water poured into her wounded hull and she slid rapidly to her grave.

A number of boats were launched before the *Mars* went down, but only one survived in the heavy swell close to the cliffs. Its six occupants — two firemen, two seamen, a cattle dealer and a young lad — kept the boat's head to the sea, and after rowing throughout the night, they reached Milford Haven. At times, they had almost given up as the strain of making progress in the semi-waterlogged boat became a nightmare. As they strained at the oars off the Linney cliffs, they were aware of a second boat being in the vicinity. But when nothing was heard of this boat the next day, it was assumed to have been swamped. One small boy is said to have climbed into a boat during the crossing and woke up to find himself alone — the boat having floated clear of the sinking steamer. But contemporary reports a week after the disaster refer only to the six survivors in one boat.

News of the loss of the *Mars* reached Waterford on the Wednesday afternoon, April 2nd, and representatives of the owners made immediate plans to travel to Milford Haven. It was already clear that about 28 passengers and 17 crewmen had been drowned. Captain Blynman, whose father had died when the *Frolic* was wrecked on Nash Sands in 1831, was among them. He had abandoned his ship at the last second, only to drown with his officers, crew and passengers among the struggling livestock.

The port of Waterford went into mourning, as family after family received word of the death of a relative or friend. One passenger left a wife and six children, the eldest of whom was eight. There was also good news for some. The families of the six survivors quietly rejoiced and those who had missed the sailing marvelled at their escape. The ship's regular mate thanked illness for forcing him to remain on shore for that voyage. Twenty-one of the dead were taken the few miles from Freshwater West to the little churchyard at Castlemartin to be buried. The burial register records that among those laid to rest was a sergeant serving in the First Battalion of the 21st Fusiliers.

The disaster had hit the pockets of Waterford merchants. One businessman had cattle on board the *Mars* worth over £1,400 and another, who was shipping poultry to Bristol, put his losses at between £60 and £70. A month after the wreck, *'The Pembrokeshire Herald'* published a memorial, in verse, to those who were lost in the disaster:

Dark came the ocean, murmuring on its way,
O'ershadowing clouds their fury spread.
And 'Mars' was dimmed, the closing day,
In darkened atmosphere arrayed.

When steering up to gain the port,
No land or beacon meets their view;
The vessel strikes, the life blood starts!
And deeply writhes the crew.

No 'Cross' had they to kneel around,
Nor Altar near to pray;
Their hearts were then in iron bound,
Beneath the rising spray.

To 'Man the boats' the seamen went,
And dared the billows wildest foams;
The breakers rolled — the cattle rent
The liquid air with moans.

My home, my home, my father land,
Dwelt sweet in every breast;
The husband grasp'd his wife's fond hand,
And sunk collaps'd in Ocean's rest.

Hurried from earth, where dear companions dwell,
To lie embossed in a sandy ore;
No more they listen to that word 'Farewell',
Breath'd, lastly breath'd, on Erin's shore.

Oh Death, thy Wings are widely spread,
Thy sickle's felt on sea and land;
Shun not the place where heroes bled,
Or shrink from death's cold hand.

From bondage free, their spirit flies
Where sudden joy appears,
To realms beyond the starry skies
In heaven's surrounded spheres.

The loss of the *Mars* was the third major shipping disaster on the Pembrokeshire coast in only six years. Only two years before, the paddle steamer *Nimrod* had gone down off St David's Head and on February 6th, 1856, the American sailing ship *Great Duke* foundered near St Govan's Head. The 2,000 ton *Great Duke*, under the command of Captain Sampson, was nearing the end of her voyage from New Orleans. It had been a stormy crossing and the crew of thirty-two were looking forward to a run ashore in Liverpool, where the cargo of 4,500 bales of cotton and other goods were to be unloaded. The violence of the south-south-westerly gale which hit the ship off the Pembrokeshire coast soon put all thoughts of the Mersey's pleasures from their minds. The storm drove the ship off course and her bowsprit struck the cliffs near Bullslaughter Bay before she grounded. In a short time, the *Great Duke* was breaking up in the heavy seas. One crewman volunteered to swim ashore with a line, but he was drowned in the wicked surf beneath the cliffs. The boatswain managed to reach the shore and climbed up the rock face beyond the high water mark. The third officer joined him and climbed even higher, but the rock gave way and he plunged to his death. Only two men — one of them the first officer — survived in the sea and they were washed ashore clinging to bales of cotton. Of the *Great Duke*'s crew of thirty-two, just three were left alive. Ironically, much of the ship's cargo of cotton and her equipment were salvaged

and, had the ship run aground a short distance to the east on the sands of Bullslaughter Bay, it is likely that all the crew would have been saved. 'The strewn wreckage, the floating bales of cotton and the carrying up of dead bodies was a sight most harrowing to behold,' wrote an eye-witness. The vigilance of the Coastguard also prevented the wreck being plundered. 'Captain Gwynne, the Inspecting Coastguard of the District was exceedingly active, owing to which, and the services of the men under his command, that restless wrecking propensity, far too prevalent along the coast, was very materially arrested,' it was reported.

The paddle steamer *Nimrod* went down off St David's Head on February 28th, 1860, and her loss remained the centre of controversy for many years. She had already hit the headlines four years before when her boiler exploded, killing six men in the engine room. At that time, she was on the Cork Steamship Company's Cork-Liverpool route, although she had also worked the service to Belfast as a relief vessel. The 600 ton *Nimrod* had been built in 1843 at

Liverpool and was the first iron packet steamer on the Cork route. She was rigged as a three-masted barque and her single-expansion steam engine gave her a top speed of ten knots.

On a Saturday morning, February 25th, 1860 she left Liverpool for Cork. Her crew and passengers totalled forty-five and she carried a general cargo, which included beer, soap, shop goods and walnuts. The voyage was just another routine trip for the *Nimrod*'s master, Captain Lyall . . . or so he thought. He had served throughout the Crimean War in one of the company's steamers and he had also been in command of its ships on the Cork-London and Liverpool-Rotterdam routes. But when the *Nimrod*'s engine broke down off the Smalls on the Monday night, February 27th, his career was racing towards a tragic conclusion. Efforts were being made to repair the engine, when the smaller Milford-Waterford packet steamer, the *City of Paris*, arrived on the scene and offered assistance. The subsequent conversation between Captain Lyall and the master of the *City of Paris*, Captain Pearn, was at the heart of the

controversy surrounding the wreck.

A statement issued after the wreck by Ford and Jackson, owners of the *City* steamer, gave this version: 'Inquiring if the *Nimrod* wanted any assistance, the reply was "What will you tow us into Milford for?" The *City of Paris* answered £1,000. The *Nimrod* offered £100. The captain of the *City of Paris* said it was out of the question, but he would tow her into Milford and leave the renumeration to be settled by the owners. This the captain of the *Nimrod* refused. The *City of Paris* remained by her for some time, but all assistance was refused by the *Nimrod*.' It was pointed out in the statement that, at the time, the weather was moderate and there was no apparent danger either to life or property. 'The wind was west, Milford Haven was quite open and St Ann's Light was visible. She had all her canvas set and good steerage way on her all the time and the only request the captain of the *Nimrod* made was for the *City of Paris* to report him at Waterford.' Captain Pearn's report was corroborated by the officers and crew of the *City of Paris*. And his company said of him: 'He has been in our employ for the last four years and a more humane and trustworthy man does not exist. We feel assured that had he for a moment contemplated the awful calamity that afterwards befell the unfortunate *Nimrod*, no thought of money would have crossed his mind. Neither, it is to be supposed, would the Captain of the *Nimrod* allowed the *City of Paris* to leave him had he foreseen the slightest danger either to himself or the passengers.'

In the event, the *City of Paris* resumed her journey and the *Nimrod* made plans to continue her crossing under sail. The whole affair might have been forgotten had not a storm blown up during the night.

The *Nimrod* was driven towards the coast of North Pembrokeshire and at eight on the Tuesday morning, February 28th, she was sighted off Ramsey Island. She had her head to windward and was drifting before the gale. Soon afterwards, she struck rocks off St David's Head and was broken into three sections. Her signals of distress had been heard in the vicinity, but would-be rescuers could only watch helplessly as the ship was driven onto rocks 200 feet below their cliff-top vantage point. As the ship struck, Captain Lyall was said to have sunk his head on the taffrail in despair. A young man kneeled, in prayer, on one of the paddle boxes and four children clung in terror to their mother. On one part of the ship, a crewman wrenched off his heavy clothes and dived into the raging sea with a lifebuoy around him. He reached wreckage and clung on, but lost his grip and cried out for help. In desperation, he struck out for more wreckage and again clung on to life but, when overcome by exhaustion, he slipped under the waves — the last of the *Nimrod*'s passengers and crew to die. No-one survived.

Disaster funds were opened at Bristol and Cork for the widows and orphans of those who had drowned. The people of North Shields also contributed to a fund for the two children of a Mrs Wigham, a passenger on the ship. Two days before the *Nimrod* had sailed, Mrs Wigham received a message that her husband, master of the vessel *Wensleydale*, had been taken ill at Queenstown. She arrived at Liverpool just in time to board the *Nimrod*, but it was a journey she never completed.

Wreckage washed ashore from the *Nimrod* included a medicine chest, two bales of black cloth, four barrels of beer, 14 boxes of soap, shop goods and a quantity of walnuts. *'The Haverfordwest and Milford Haven Telegraph'* suggested that as the people of the St David's area had 'the best share of profit' from the wreck, they should subscribe liberally to the disaster funds. A letter in the same newspaper claimed that 'most conspicuous in appropriating the portion of the wreck that came ashore to their own purpose were those who were distinguished by the profession of religion'.

Investigations into the cause of the loss of the *Nimrod* were obviously hampered by the absence of any survivors. The Board of Trade accepted the statement of explanation issued by the owners of the *City of Paris* and a letter from one of that ship's passengers, a Captain Driver, also showed that no blame was attached to Captain Pearn. Captain Driver had stated: 'At the time the ships parted, the *Nimrod* had all Lights open to Milford Haven and a fair wind, and the *Nimrod*'s captain thought he could make Milford Haven without assistance. But after the vessels parted, the wind changed and blew with such violence that the *City of Paris* did not make seven knots in three hours. She would then have been completely unable to render assistance to the *Nimrod*, as it was as much as she could do to maintain her own position.' Officially, the *Nimrod* affair was closed, but it has remained a controversial issue.

One of the worst multiple shipwrecks on the county's coastline occurred six years later during one of those November storms which frequently wreak havoc across Pembrokeshire. About eight ships were in company in the Bristol Channel running for the shelter of Milford Haven on the night of Saturday, November 10th, 1866. Torrential rain seriously reduced visibility in the darkness and the first ship ran aground in Mill Bay at the entrance to the Haven. The others — on the same course — followed her in and soon fell prey to the waves and the rocks. The bay became a mass of hulks and wreckage and the cries for help were heard by the men manning the lighthouse on St Ann's Head. They raced to the cliffs above the bay and saved fourteen seamen from the 'very jaws of death'. Another eight sailors got away in an open boat and landed at Dale.

At first, it was difficult to distinguish ship from ship in the wreckage and it was some days before a true picture emerged. By then, a number of bodies had been washed ashore on neighbouring beaches. The barque *Commodore*, of Rye, on a voyage from Swansea to London with patent fuel, was extensively damaged, but all her crew were saved. The Truro schooner *Isobel* — from Neath to Plymouth with coal — was a total wreck. Only her captain and one seaman survived and both received a severe battering, with their bodies covered in bruises and gashes from the rocks. The schooner *King of the Forest* was also wrecked, but part of her cargo of railway iron was salvaged. She was bound from Cardiff to Liverpool and all her hands were saved. A third schooner, the *Hope*, whose home port was Poole, broke up with her cargo of coal and her captain and a boy died in the wreck. Two of her crew survived. Of the other ships, only two could be identified — the *Alfred Eliza* and the *Eliza and Jane*.

The smack *Alfred Eliza* was from the French port of Rouville and was carrying coal. Her crew, and those of the *Eliza and Jane*, were rescued. Many of the bodies which were recovered were buried at Dale, but they went unidentified because of the confusion of that terrible night.

In April, 1943, two landing craft were caught in a fierce gale as they tried to reach Milford Haven for shelter. Both craft were swamped by heavy seas and seventy-eight men died, including six from a rescue boat. The disaster shocked the nation, but because of wartime censorship, the full facts did not emerge until much later. Indeed, at the time, the craft were described as barges, because of secrecy surrounding these LCGs — landing craft gun designed to engage the enemy's shore defences during the invasion of Sicily. *LCGs 15* and *16*, each of 627 tons, had been the first to be converted at Belfast for their new role. However, to save time, only a partial deck had been fitted and a large open space was left behind the sealed-off bow ramp — a feature which was to prove fatal. The two craft sailed for Holyhead to take on supplies and then headed down the coast of Wales on a course for Falmouth. Each LCG carried a naval commander and crew, and a large contingent of Royal Marines to operate the two 4.7 inch guns and twin Oerlikons. The complements of both craft totalled 75 officers and men.

It was Easter Sunday, April 25th, when the weather deteriorated. A deep depression had developed much sooner than expected and the commanding officers of the two craft decided they could make Milford Haven. *LCG 15* arrived off St Ann's Head at mid-day. A full onshore gale was blowing, with a heavy and confused sea, and her attempts to reach shelter were frustrated by the conditions. *LCG 16* was out of sight of her sister craft and both had shipped tremendous seas which 'ponded' in the open area behind the blunt bow.

Late that afternoon, *LCG 15* lost her battle. She foundered off the coast between Sheep Island and Freshwater West in sight of hundreds of rescuers, who watched, in horror, as those on board were drowned or battered to death against the razor-sharp rocks. There were no survivors. Among the ships sent out to aid the landing craft was the escort sloop *H.M.S. Rosemary*, which attempted to get a tow line to the surviving *LCG 16*. After several attempts failed, six sailors volunteered to take a line across to the landing craft in a whaler. Within minutes of the boat being launched it was swamped and all six were swept to their deaths. Angle Lifeboat was off-service for an overhaul, so it was the St David's Lifeboat, *Sŵn-y-Môr*, which was alerted that night. She was launched, with Coxswain William Watts Williams in command, at 10.45 p.m. and faced an 18-mile haul, in the south-westerly gale and heavy seas, to reach Milford Haven. The knowledge that there were floating mines in the area added to the difficulties of the service. The lifeboat reached the area off St Ann's Head at one in the morning. There was a strong smell of oil and the sea was now smoother, but they saw nothing. The search was continued and 40 minutes later, she picked up a man who was covered in oil and was in a bad way. He was stripped of his clothing, massaged and re-clothed in an emergency suit and then put in the engine room, with bags as a pillow and an oilskin coat as a blanket.

The Royal Navy escort sloop 'H.M.S. Rosemary', which lost six of her crew in the bid to save the men of the landing craft 'LCG 16' in April, 1943. (Picture: Wright & Logan).

LCG 16 had foundered sometime after midnight and the search for survivors went on until daylight. At one stage, the lifeboat nearly ran on to a mine and missed destruction by only a few yards. The St David's Lifeboat arrived back at her station at 8.30 a.m., after a rough passage. Coxswain Watts Williams had been at the wheel for nearly ten hours and now faced the problem of re-housing the boat in the heavy seas on the slipway. He decided to take the risk and the lifeboat was successfully hauled up the slip, with hardly any damage. One survivor of *LCG 16* was taken to the home of Dr Joseph Soar, the honorary lifeboat secretary. Later, an ambulance took the

War graves at Milford Haven Cemetery include those of 39 of the 78 men who lost their lives in the landing craft disaster in April, 1943. (Picture: Malcolm Richards).

man, a naval stoker, to Milford Haven, where he joined two other survivors from the landing craft — a Royal Marines officer and a sergeant, who had both been washed ashore. Seventy-two men from *LCGs 15* and *16* had been lost and six men had drowned from *H.M.S. Rosemary*'s whaler. Over fifty bodies were recovered and thirty-nine were buried in a mass grave at Milford Haven Cemetery.

The death of so many men caused considerable concern and there were questions in Parliament. One M.P., C. G. Ammon, asked the First Lord of the Admiralty, A. V. Alexander, whether he would make a statement on the disaster. Well over a month later, Mr Alexander told the House of Commons:

'The Board of Inquiry has completed its full investigations, and the results have been carefully examined by the Admiralty. For operational reasons alone I cannot go into the full details of the unfortunate loss of the two vessels off Milford Haven. I can, however, assure the House that in the findings of the Board there is no question of the disaster being attributable to negligence. The fundamental cause of the tragedy at Milford Haven was that the weather changed suddenly, in spite of favourable forecasts. A deep depression came over at a speed far greater than expected. In spite of modern science, circumstances of this nature do sometimes arise, and it was unfortunate that on this occasion these barges encountered a high wind and sea, and an unfavourable tide in a difficult and dangerous area. The vessels were sailed in good weather and with the prospects favourable, but, unhappily, the weather after a sudden change deteriorated with a rapidity unusual, even for St George's Channel. The commanding officers, nevertheless, decided that they could make Milford Haven. They arrived off the place at mid-day on April 25th. By this time conditions were severe, with a full gale blowing onshore and with a heavy and confused sea.

'The Flag Officer in charge at Milford Haven at once took steps to secure that every possible attempt was made to bring these craft safely into harbour. He sent two tugs and two trawlers to their assistance, and diverted *H.M.S. Rosemary*, an escort vessel, which was in the area, to the scene. These vessels did all in their power in most dangerous and difficult conditions to help the barges to safety. They succeeded in passing a tow several times, but owing to the heavy seas the tow parted on each occasion. Finally, the barges foundered. In spite of all the strenuous and gallant efforts by the rescue ships seventy-two members of the crews of the barges lost their lives, as well as the six members of the crew of *Rosemary*'s whaler, which was launched in a courageous attempt to pick up survivors.'

Mr Ammon pointed out that it was alleged in the neighbourhood that the accident could have been prevented had the officers on the spot had authority to cancel the instructions. But Alexander replied: 'There is no word of truth in any suggestion of that kind. The commanding officers had full instructions on what to do in certain circumstances, and the Flag Officer on the spot took every possible step.'

The day after the disaster, Coxswain Watts Williams and the crew of the St David's Lifeboat were sent a message of thanks from the Flag Officer at Milford Haven for 'their prompt answer to our call and admiration for their efforts during the rescue'. Coxswain Watts Williams was later awarded the R.N.L.I.'s bronze medal for his gallantry during this service. The citation referred to his devotion to duty in difficult conditions and his great skill in re-housing the lifeboat. He and the seven members of his crew received additional monetary awards, as did the four launchers who assisted in re-housing the lifeboat.

The non-availability of the Angle Lifeboat was a situation which the R.N.L.I. had always feared would arrive one day. During the Second World War, the Institution was strained to fill the gaps when a lifeboat was off service for an overhaul. Some of the lifeboats had been lost by enemy action, others had been requisitioned by the Government; and some waited, half-built, in yards for men to complete them. The R.N.L.I.'s fear was that the time would come when there would be no reserve boat in a major emergency and this is exactly what happened at Angle. There was no reserve boat to replace the Angle Lifeboat and when the Admiralty wrote about the landing craft disaster, it was reminded that the R.N.L.I. had begged for men to complete its half-built boats and had been told that they could not be spared. Had there been a lifeboat at Angle that night, many more men might well have been saved.

The U-Boat Menace

A whitewashed farmhouse on the North Pembrokeshire coast returned vividly to his memory whenever Captain Anton Sonné recalled his career at sea during the First World War. The captain had been born and brought up in Vaasa, a Finnish timber port on the Gulf of Bothnia and first went to sea as a messboy on a Swedish steamer. But this working holiday trip convinced young Anton to turn seaman full-time. After a transatlantic voyage in the Norwegian barque *Queen of Grimstad* in the spring of 1915, he signed on the *Formosa*, which was preparing to leave Liverpool to load a cargo of timber in Novia Scotia.

The lovely little barque *Formosa*, which was also sailing under the Norwegian flag, was known for her fast voyages. And on the return run across the North Atlantic on a strong north-westerly gale, she made the Irish port of Cork in 14 days. But as she headed up the Pembrokeshire coast back to Liverpool on Friday, November 12th, she ran into one of the worst gales her captain

had ever experienced. Captain Frederick Eriksen sent the crew aloft to reduce sail to lower tops'ls — an operation which took hours in the nightmare conditions. When the weather seemed to be improving, the mainsail was set again. But soon afterwards, the ship was hit by a killer squall which shifted the deck cargo and blew out all sail. Huge seas swept over the ship, which was now drifting helplessly in the darkness on a lee shore. Desperate efforts were made to rig spare sail and just as it looked as though they were out of danger the wind changed direction again, driving the *Formosa* on to a submerged rock off the North Bishops. Within minutes the ship began to fill. Her fore and main topmasts had broken and were over the side and her sails were torn to ribbons in the shrieking wind. Heavy seas lashed her deck, smashing everything in their path and flooding the cabin and deckhouse. With no hope of saving his ship, Captain Eriksen ordered his men into the two boats in a bid to reach safety. It was now ten o'clock on the morning of the 13th. The *Formosa*'s plight had not gone unnoticed ashore. She had been sighted drifting towards the rocks by

Coxswain Ivor Arnold, of the St David's Lifeboat, and he launched the *General Farrell* with a full crew at about 10.30 a.m.

The lifeboat got alongside the wreck, which by now was awash at the stern and labouring heavily, despite her timber cargo. When he found the crew had abandoned ship, Coxswain Arnold headed the lifeboat northward and found one of the *Formosa*'s boats carrying eleven men. There was no sign of the second boat, which had been manned by Captain Eriksen and six of his crew, including Anton Sonné. The eleven survivors transferred to the lifeboat, which arrived back at its St David's station, with the *Formosa*'s boat in tow, at 2 p.m. The missing boat, meanwhile, had headed for neighbouring Whitesands Bay in the hope of beaching safely on the sands. But the strong current kept carrying the boat towards the rocks and as they rowed for their lives, Anton Sonné glimpsed the whitewashed farmhouse, looking so desirable, ashore. They managed to pull away from the rocks, but surf breaking on the beach overturned the boat and Anton was trapped beneath it. He fought his way free and reached the shore

safely with the captain and the other five crew members. Later, they joined the remainder of the survivors at St David's, where they were welcomed by the local Lloyd's agent, W. Arnold. Anton Sonné went on to a distinguished career at sea but he never forgot the *Formosa* and the white-washed farmhouse on that foreign shore.

Further along the coast at Fishguard Harbour, other seamen were also counting the cost of the storm. The Milford fishing ketch *Flora* had been left a total wreck under French Walk, with the Cardiff coaster *Emlyn* resting against her hulk. Three other steamers, the *Echo*, of Bristol; the *Dinorwic*, of Caernarvon, and the *Cautiose*, were aground on Goodwick Beach, and other ships which had sought shelter in the bay were also damaged. The crew of the *Flora* went through a harrowing ordeal in that Saturday storm. As tremendous seas swept over the little ketch, they lashed themselves to the rigging and it was eight hours before they were finally brought ashore by breeches buoy. The captain and crew of the *Emlyn* were rescued by the Fishguard Lifeboat, *Charterhouse*. Later that morning,

Coxswain John Howells took the lifeboat out again, to the aid of the three-masted barque *Calburga* — which, like the *Formosa*, had been bound for Liverpool with Nova Scotia timber.

The barque — her sails and two masts gone — had first been sighted off Strumble Head by the incoming Fishguard-Rosslare steamer *Great Southern*. But the stricken ship was too close to the rocks for the steamer to approach. When the lifeboat reached the barque, she had already run on to rocks at Pen Brush and was breaking up. At first it was thought her captain and crew of thirteen had perished, but it was later learned that their boat had landed safely three miles away at Aber-Bach. The shipwrecked mariners were lucky to be alive. The First World War had already brought with it enough hazards and the storm came at the back end of a black year for shipping using routes off the Pembrokeshire coast. Indeed, an omen of what was in store arrived early in the war with three shipwrecks within a month.

On August 15th, 1914 — ten days after war was declared — the British cargo ship *Ellerbeck* ran aground on the notorious Hats and Barrels rocks near the Smalls lighthouse. The 1,499 tons steamship had been launched only four years before and was on passage from Barry to Pentland with a cargo of coal. Her signals of distress were sighted from the mainland and the St David's Lifeboat *General Farrell* went to her aid.

Part of the *Ellerbeck*'s crew, who had taken to boats, were picked up by the lifeboat, but her captain and ten volunteers decided to stay on board, aiming to get the ship off the rocks on spring tides a few days later. The forepart of the steamer was already filling with water, however, and the rocks had penetrated the engine room. When the Milford trawler *Avonmouth* arrived on the scene she found the ship in a perilous position and rocking ominously. The captain and his volunteers now had no choice but to abandon ship and they were brought into Milford Haven by the fishing smack *Monarch*. The other crew members were taken to St David's, having remained in the lifeboat. The *Ellerbeck* became a total wreck — another victim of the Hats and Barrels.

A week later, the Brixham trawler, *Alpha*, sailed from Milford Haven for the Cardigan Bay fishing grounds. But her trip ended north of St David's Head when she ran onto rocks in thick fog. Her skipper, Fred Tucker, and his crew of three, took to the trawler's boat and rowed safely to shore. The third ship to hit trouble was the Sunderland steamship *Endcliffe*, which was carrying 300 tons of scrap iron from Preston to Llanelli. She struck rocks off the little North Pembrokeshire port of Porthgain on September 6th in fog. Her captain was able to bring her off the rocks, stern first, and headed down the coast to beach her at Porthmelgan just below St David's Head. The crew removed their belongings and moveable deck fittings and the ship was later successfully refloated after temporary repairs.

In January, 1915, a German submarine — Otto Hersing's *U-21* — made a pilot raid into the Irish Sea, after slipping through the English Channel defences. It marked the beginning of a terror campaign against merchant shipping unprecedented in the history of warfare. Pembrokeshire, so strategically placed to command the main shipping routes, played a major part in the fight against the U-boats. The county also became a refuge for the hundreds of survivors from ships which fell victim to the German submarines.

By the end of March, 1915, the 16 U-boats then on operational patrol in British waters had sunk 28,000 tons of shipping. And the shocks of the war at sea hit home for the people of Pembrokeshire on successive days — March 27th and 28th — when the liners *Aguila* and *Falaba* were torpedoed by Baron von Forstner's *U-28*.

The ships were sunk well off the Pembrokeshire coast — the *Aguila* going down 47 miles south-west of the Smalls, and the *Falaba* 38 miles west of that position — but Milford Haven and Fishguard became reception centres for the crews and passengers. The Yeoward Bros. steamship *Aguila* was on a voyage to Lisbon and the Canary Islands when she was sighted and chased by *U-28*. The liner increased speed to 14 knots but was soon overhauled by the submarine and compelled to stop after a shot had been fired across her bows.

While boats were being lowered, the U-boat began shelling the vessel. The chief engineer and two men were killed and 20 shells struck the ship before a torpedo split her in half. Eight lives were lost in the attack, including a woman passenger and a stewardess who drowned when one of the liner's boats capsized. The thirty-eight survivors, who included the captain, were picked up by the steamer *St Stephen*, and the trawler *Ottilie* which put into Fishguard.

Von Forstner struck again the following day. The Elder Dempster liner *Falaba* was on passage from Liverpool to Sierra Leone when the U-boat ordered her to stop. She responded by increasing speed, but when a second signal was received ordering — 'Stop or I will fire into you' — the *Falaba* hove to, knowing the submarine could outpace the ship. The passengers and crew began abandoning ship, but only five boats had been swung out when *U-28* fired a torpedo into the liner without warning. Of the one hundred and fifty-one passengers and ninety-six crew, one hundred and four died — either by drowning or in the explosion when the torpedo struck. Survivors arriving at Milford Haven spoke of the German submariners laughing and jeering as their victims struggled in the water. Those who had been sucked under when the liner sank, bobbed to the surface desperately attempting to grab at wreckage to stay afloat.

The drifter *Eileen Emma* played a leading part in the rescue operations and her skipper, George Wright, was awarded a piece of plate by the Board of Trade in recognition of his services.

At John Cory's 'Sailors Rest and Bethel' at Milford Haven, a tablet was later erected to commemorate the crews of the torpedoed ships, and particular reference was made to the men, women and children saved from the *Falaba*. Among those lost in the disaster was an American citizen, Leon Thresher. His death caused a storm of protest in the United States and further losses of American lives, including those who went down with the liner *Lusitania*, finally resulted in the U.S.A. entering the war against Germany in 1917.

Attacks on merchant shipping continued throughout 1915, although the U-boats were reluctant to venture too close to the

Pembrokeshire coast. On June 8th, the three-masted schooner *Express*, of 115 tons, was stopped and sunk by a submarine 44 miles south-south-west of the Smalls. The *Express* was a former wooden paddle steamer built in 1883 and later converted to sail. The same day, the sailing vessel *Susannah* fell victim to the U-boat and four days later the barques *Crown of India* and *Bellglade* were attacked by *U-35*.

The *Crown of India* — a four-masted barque of Liverpool — was bound from Barry to Pernambuco, Brazil, with a cargo of coal. The submarine put nine shells into her and she went down stern first with all sails set — 'a fine but distressing spectacle' for her captain, Colin Branch, and his crew. Their boats were picked up by the Milford steam trawler *Queen Alexandra* and the barque's only casualties were her two cats which went down with the vessel.

The *Bellglade*, of Tönsberg, Norway, was nearing the end of her voyage to Sharpness with a cargo of timber from Halifax, Nova Scotia. Her captain and crew saw the *Crown of India* under attack and knew they would be the U-boat's next victim. But after putting three shots into the *Bellglade*'s hull, the submarine submerged when the trawler *Queen Alexandra* approached. She took off the barque's crew and the *Bellglade* was later towed into Milford Haven after being found floating keel uppermost.

Before the month was out, the steamships *Strathnairn* and *Indrani* had been sunk off the coast, as well as another barque, the

The 'Crown of India', a four-masted barque sunk by 'U-35' in June, 1915. Her crew were rescued by the Milford steam trawler 'Queen Alexandra'.
(Picture: National Maritime Museum).

101

Dumfriesshire, whose crew was brought into Milford Haven by the trawler *Weymouth*. As they walked from the docks they were described as 'a pitiful spectacle hatless, most of them bootless and few fully clothed'.

As the summer wore on, hardly a week went by without Press reports of 'more murders by pirates'. On July 9th, the steamer *Ellesmere*, of Manchester and the Russian tanker *Ito* were torpedoed with the loss of eight lives. In August, Max Valentiner and his *U-38* sank twenty-two steamers, three sailing vessels and five fishing boats in the Irish Sea. The ships included the steamship *Thornfield* and the colliers, *Glenby* and *The Queen*, which all went down north of the Smalls.

The winter storms of 1915 which wreaked havoc on Allied shipping, also kept the U-boats at bay. Although, in an isolated attack in December, the 3,284 ton ship *Van Stirum* was torpedoed off the Smalls on Christmas Day, with the loss of two lives.

The Royal Navy base at Milford Haven suffered a severe blow that month when three of its patrol drifters foundered in the gales. The *Susanna* sank on the 14th and the *Ladysmith* and *Ferndale* on the 27th.

Chief officer Albert Mockridge, of the St Ann's Head Coastguards, saw the little *Ferndale* turn into the Haven in a very heavy sea. One of her crew was washed overboard and soon afterwards the drifter struck the rocks below the Head and quickly broke up. Attempts had been made to get a line to the vessel but the wind was so strong that the rocket apparatus was blown away.

On the last day of the year, the collier *Satrap*, on hire to the Admiralty, foundered on the South Pembrokeshire coast, near Manorbier, with the loss of all hands. The ship was owned by the Trident Line, of Newport (Mon.) and had sailed from Barry. A memorial plaque in Manorbier Church recognises 'the kindness and Christian treatment accorded to the departed, their relatives and the owners by the Vicar and the parishioners'.

A change of policy by Germany on U-boat warfare, to avoid further friction with the neutral United States, resulted in a dramatic drop in shipping losses, particularly off Pembrokeshire. However, minelaying submarines were posing a new terror for the merchantmen. The steamer *Kelvinia* was lost nine miles off Caldey Island after striking a mine on September 2nd. Three weeks later the minesweeper *H.M.S. Loch Shiel* blew up and sank off Milford Haven. It was believed that she either struck a mine or one became entangled in her sweeps as they were being hauled in. Nine of the crew of this former Aberdeen trawler were rescued by a patrol boat. Three men were killed.

Earlier in the year, the Admiralty lost another patrol drifter when the *Pecheur* sank after a collision off the Smalls on April 3rd. In October, 1916, the German authorities gave the go-ahead for a new campaign against enemy shipping. But it was not until December 26th that a U-boat launched an attack close to the Pembrokeshire coast. Her victim was the sailing vessel *Agnes*, which was ordered to stop and was sunk by a bomb, after the crew had got safely away in the ship's boat. From February, 1917, U-boats were ordered to wage unrestricted war on merchant ships and sinkings rose alarmingly. Anti-submarine measures seemed hopelessly inadequate. A hydro-phone station had been set up on St David's Head early in the war, but there is little evidence that it proved particularly successful. Shortages of destroyers and patrol craft, and the painfully slow development of the depth charge, added to Britain's difficulties as ship after ship was sent to the bottom by the submarines.

One of the first casualties of the U-boats' new campaign in the Irish Sea was the Liverpool steamer *Voltaire*, which was cleared of food and provisions by the German boarding party before being sunk. The *Voltaire*'s captain and crew were picked up by a Glasgow ship and landed at Fishguard. The same day, February 11th, 1917, the Cornish coaster *Olivia* and the armed merchantman *Lycia* were sunk 25 miles north of the South Bishop. And the following day, the tanker *Pinna* was beached at Milford Haven, after twice being torpedoed. For services to the tanker, the owners, master and crew of the tug *Margaret Ham* received £750.

Fishing smacks were particularly vulnerable to U-boat attacks. On February 13th the smack *Zircon* was sunk 26 miles south-west of the Smalls during a heavy gale. Skipper F. Sutton and his crew of five took to their boat and were finally picked up by a pilot cutter off the Irish coast. They had no food or water and were all suffering from frost-bite and exposure. Their attacker also destroyed the Milford-owned smack *Friendship*, off the Smalls, with the loss of the skipper and crew of three. U-boats were now venturing closer and closer to the Pembrokeshire coast. On February 14th, the 3,050 ton cargo ship *Inishowen Head* was torpedoed only one-and-a-quarter miles off Skokholm Island. She was owned by the Ulster Steamship Company, of Belfast, who were leaders in operating fast cargo traffic services on the North Atlantic. The *Inishowen Head* had been launched in 1886 and was the company's first steel ship. No warning was given by the German submarine of the attack and the ship went down very quickly. One crewman died in the incident and the thirty-six survivors spent four hours in an open boat in the bitterly cold weather before landing safely near Marloes.

The following day the *Afton* was captured and sunk by bombs north of Strumble Head and on the 26th, the brigantine *Hannah Croasdell* struck a mine and sank four miles off St Ann's Head with the loss of four lives.

The previous week, the Leyland Line, of Liverpool, suffered a severe blow when their 4,703 tons cargo ship *Leysian* was wrecked seven miles off Strumble Head. She was on a voyage in ballast from Belfast to Cardiff. Her thirty-nine crew members took to their boats and were later picked up by the Fishguard Lifeboat, *Charterhouse*. In a second wreck within four days, another cargo ship, the *Cymric Prince*, owned by the Anglo-Belgique Shipping Company, sank after running onto the North Bishop rocks. She was carrying iron ore to Hartlepool.

As winter slowly gave way to spring, the slaughter of ships by U-boats continued. On March 1st. the liner *Drina*, which was on hire to the Admiralty as a hospital ship, was torpedoed two miles off Skokholm. Fifteen men died in the attack. The four-masted barque *Inverlogie* was sunk 15 miles south-west of the Smalls and later that March, tragedy struck a number of Milford Haven homes when the minesweeping trawler *Evangel* sank after hitting a mine off the port.

The four-masted barque 'Inverlogie', torpedoed 15 miles south-west of the Smalls in March, 1917.

(Picture: National Maritime Museum).

Insurance premiums for shipping rose sharply as the sinkings mounted. The famous three-masted iron barque *Borrowdale* carried war risk insurance of £18,000 when she sailed from Newport (Mon) in the April. Her voyage ended at the mouth of the Bristol Channel where she was sunk by a U-boat. Her crew managed to reach Milford Haven safely in their own boats. The sailing vessel *William Shepherd* and the coaster *Dantzig* met the same fate, fortunately without loss of life. Anti-submarines measures during the war included the hire of Q-ships — decoy vessels which appeared easy prey for U-boats. In fact, they were equipped with hidden armament. One of these mystery ships was the Milford fishing smack *Strumble*, which carried one 12-pounder gun. She entered active service in June, 1916, but less than a year later — on May 4th — she was sunk off Strumble Head by *U-65*.

The *Strumble*'s parent ship at Milford Haven was the yacht, *H.M.S. Idaho*, commanded by Lieutenant-Commander Charles E. Evans, RNVR. He was a prolific writer who had a fund of stories about his

The figurehead of the 'Borrowdale', a three-masted iron barque sunk by a U-boat off South Pembrokeshire in 1917.
(Picture: National Maritime Museum).

service at the Pembrokeshire port. He recalled the pluck of one group of survivors from a torpedoed ship:

'They were very weak when they landed at the pier but raised a cheer for their rescuers. Very few of our service had any underclothing left; they had bestowed it practically all on torpedoed crews and passengers. Of the crew I speak of, thirteen had taken refuge on the keel of the lifeboat, nine on a raft, while the captain and chief officer were picked up from separate pieces of wreckage.

'The U-boat came alongside the upturned lifeboat and one of the men swam to it and asked permission to stand on the submarine's deck and right the lifeboat. The only reply was a pistol levelled at his head and "Get out, you swine". When my friend rescued them, they had been three-and-a-half hours in icy cold water. Four of the men on the raft had died of exposure, but the survivors were singing "Keep the Home Fires Burning", while some distance away the men clinging to the keel of the lifeboat were singing "Tipperary". The chief officer, on his piece of wreckage, was singing a song of his own, but they couldn't make out the tune.'

It was believed that the U-boats were receiving help from the shore. Lieutenant-Commander Evans thought that signals flashed across the Haven were being repeated from the south side to submarines, who were given intelligence on shipping movements at the port. The captain of a merchant ship torpedoed off the Pembrokeshire coast was taken on board one German submarine and shown a copy of a British newspaper published the previous day!

The attack on the Q-ship *Strumble* was followed by the sinking of the fishing smack *Victorious*.

That month, the Leyland Line lost a second ship off Pembrokeshire, when the *Colonian* was wrecked on the North Bishop while on passage from Boston to London. A week later, the Admiralty collier *Bestwood* sank after a collision 12 miles south-west of the South Bishop lighthouse.

A two-month lull in U-boat attacks ended on successive days in August. The fishing smack *Gloriosa* was destroyed 12 miles south-by-west of Caldey Island and another fishing vessel, the *Eleazer*, was shelled and sunk 25 miles off St Ann's Head. Among the German minelaying submarines which operated off Pembrokeshire was the *UC-51* which, on September 15th, torpedoed the French steamship *Saint Jacques* some miles off the entrance to Milford Haven. It was probably a mine laid by this U-boat which sank another Admiralty patrol drifter, *Active III*, on October 15th, with the loss of all hands, some of whom were local men. A month later, however, the *UC-51* was herself sunk in the North Sea.

The area off Skokholm was a favourite haunt of the U-boats and on October 3rd, the Clyde Shipping Company's armed merchantman, *Hurst*, was torpedoed two miles off the island, without loss of life.

During the autumn of 1917, the steamship *Ionian* returned to trooping duties under the banner of Canadian Pacific Ocean Services. She was operated commercially for

The steamship 'Ionian' – torpedoed off St. Govan's Head by a German U-boat in October, 1917.

(Picture: Real Photographs).

part of the war and had escaped disaster in the English Channel when in March, 1917, she was attacked by a submarine. But the torpedo missed its target. When she sailed from Milford Haven on October 20th, however, she had only an hour of her useful life left. She was torpedoed two miles west of St Govan's Head and drifted ashore near Huntsman's Leap. All one hundred and sixty men in the ship, which had been struck in the engine room, got safely away in the boats. But as they attempted to land, one of the boats overturned and its twenty-two occupants were flung into the sea.

Six of the men drowned and the remainder spent the night clinging to rocks. A farmer found the survivors the next morning and took them to hospital at Pembroke Dock ten miles away. The *Ionian*'s other boats had rowed back to Milford Haven, burning flares to attract attention, but they were near the entrance to the port before they were rescued by a patrol boat. An inquest on the six men was held at a farm near St Govan's and they were buried in the little graveyard at Castlemartin Church. Their graves are among the many of war victims at cemeteries throughout the county. The wreck of the *Ionian* still lies at the base of the cliffs. Recent hydrographic surveys located her boilers and engines and quantities of torn steel plating.

Four more ships were torpedoed off the coast before the end of the year. The collier *Gisella* went down off Skokholm on November 18th, with the loss of two lives. A second collier, the *Charleston*, was sunk 30 miles west of the Smalls on December 12th and two of her gunners were taken prisoner by the U-boat. A few days before Christmas, the 2,120 ton merchantman *Colemore* was torpedoed off the Smalls and five men died. A third collier, the *Lord Derby*, was lost seven miles off St Ann's Head on December 28th and all but three of her crew survived the attack.

During the closing months of 1917, there were signs that the tide was turning against the U-boats. The introduction of the convoy system began to stem shipping losses and the entry of America into the war had brought destroyers to boost the anti-submarine patrols. It was also now possible to detect the presence and exact position of most German U-boats by an elaborate system of radio stations, one of which was at Milford Haven.

One of the first casualties of 1918 was the Belgian steam trawler, *John* but not as a result of enemy action. She sank off the Smalls after a collision with another Belgian trawler, *Count Van De Burgh*. Six of the *John*'s crew died in the incident and the trawler went down in three minutes after an explosion in the engine room. Later, at an inquest at Milford Haven, it was revealed that only one man had been on watch on the *Count Van De Burgh* at the time — there should have been at least two. The previous day, the steamship *Boston City* had been torpedoed 11 miles off St Ann's Head. But it was not until late in February that a U-boat found another victim — this time the cargo ship *Renfrew*. Her captain and thirty-nine crew members were killed when the ship was torpedoed eight miles off Milford Haven.

Two sailing vessels were sunk on successive days in March — the *Jane Gray* and *John G. Walter* — and five ships were lost in April. The steamship *Boscastle* was torpedoed 14 miles north of Strumble Head, with the loss of the captain and seventeen of the crew; the sailing ship *Wilson* was sunk off the Smalls; and the *Landonia* went down well north of Strumble, twenty-one of her seamen being killed and her captain taken prisoner. A few days later the sailing vessel *Ethel* was shelled and destroyed off the Smalls and the cargo ship *Gresham* was torpedoed in the vicinity. The Admiralty also lost another of its patrol drifters, when on April 16th the *Select* sank after a collision off St Govan's Head.

May saw just two losses off the Pembrokeshire coast — the collier *Baron Ailsa*, on hire to the Admiralty, and the *Wileysike*. The collier was torpedoed 18 miles west-north-west of the Smalls and went down in less than a minute with the loss of ten men. The survivors were picked up by a destroyer and landed at Milford Haven. Four men died when the *Wileysike* sank.

The first American ship to go down off the coast during the war was the coastguard cutter *USS Tampa*. She was torpedoed in the Bristol Channel on September 26th with the loss of all hands and one of her crew is buried in the churchyard at the South Pembrokeshire village of Lamphey. Earlier that summer, the cargo ship *Vandalia* had been torpedoed off the Smalls, and within three days in August the steamships *Virent* and *Ant Cassar* fell victim to a U-boat. In September the *Serula* was sunk 13 miles north of Strumble Head, with the deaths of her captain and sixteen crewmen. As the war wound wearily to its conclusion, tragedy still stalked the seas off Pembrokeshire. Bodies were washed ashore from the Japanese liner *Hirano Maru*, which had been torpedoed on October 4th in a strong gale off the Irish coast. Only twenty-eight people were saved from her ninety-seven passengers and one hundred and forty-three crew.

On the 16th of that month, the steamship *Pentwyn* was sunk 20 miles north of the South Bishop and four days later — with the signing of the Armistice only weeks away — the little sailing vessel *Emily Millington* became the U-boats' final victim of the war in Pembrokeshire waters. She was captured and sunk by gunfire, fortunately without loss of life.

At November victory celebrations at Milford Haven, tributes were paid to the two hundred and fifty men from the port's naval base who had won honours for action against the German submarines. And on December 22nd, one of the vanquished foe — *U-112* — was towed into Milford Haven to go on view to the public at sixpence a time!

The cargo ship 'Renfrew' (formerly the 'Galavale'), which was torpedoed eight miles off St. Ann's Head in February, 1918, with the loss of 40 lives.

Air Attack

The summer was at its height but the little steamship *Thorold* faced a rough sea as she headed for London with her vital cargo of best Welsh coal. She had been born for service on the Canadian Lakes eighteen years before, but had been later bought by Newcastle owners and now operated under wartime conditions. Two miles to the north lay the Smalls lighthouse, clearly visible on that August morning in 1940 in the fresh north-westerly breeze. Captain H. Jackson and his crew of fourteen were working up an appetite for lunch, not knowing that the end was nigh for some of them. The end of the *Thorold* and some of her crew came swiftly, as three German bombers dived in for the attack. The first bombs smashed the little ship's bridge and her radio room, and others penetrated one of her holds. Then the aircraft circled the dying ship for an hour machine-gunning the crew. When the bombers finally flew off the ship was sinking.

News of the attack reached coastguards on the mainland of Pembrokeshire shortly after 11.30 a.m. and the naval authorities gave permission for the St David's Lifeboat to be launched. The go-ahead was received by the honorary secretary of the St David's station, Dr Joseph Soar, who decided to join the boat on her mercy mission. When the lifeboat hit the waters of Ramsey Sound it was 12.40 p.m. and she headed for the last known position of the *Thorold*. Contact was kept by radio with the Smalls lighthouse and the lifeboat was given a course, as the crippled ship had by now completely disappeared. In the rough seas, it was difficult to see any sign of the *Thorold*'s boats and rafts. But after about three miles one of the lifeboatmen saw a jacket on a pole — a signal from survivors. The lifeboat altered course, guided by this signal from a raft, and on the way found a man clinging to a plank. It was the master, Captain Jackson. His head was cut open, one of his legs was broken, and with loss of blood and several hours spent in the sea he was scarcely living. Yet he clung so desperately to the plank that lifeboatmen D. Lewis and G. Davies had to go into the sea to force open his grip and help him into the lifeboat. The second engineer was found on another piece of wreckage, and on the raft were thirteen men still alive out of the crew of twenty-four. One was the mate, who had broken a leg and was barely alive.

The lifeboat turned for home, radioing through the Smalls lighthouse for doctors and ambulances to be ready when she arrived. The crew of the lifeboat did what they could for the survivors, giving them rum, rubbing their numbed limbs and covering them with oilskins. For a time Captain Jackson rallied. Then he collapsed and died. The mate lived a little longer, only to die when the lifeboat reached the shore.

The *Thorold* was one of the first victims of German air attacks on shipping off the Pembrokeshire coast. Until June 1940, reaching the area by air from Germany was almost out of the question. But when France fell the picture changed dramatically. Raids on commerce were pressed home by the Luftwaffe's Heinkel IIIs, Junkers 88s and Dorniers, with the occasional Focke-Wulf 200 — the Kondor — launching an attack after prowling far out into the Atlantic. U-boats played little part in the destruction of shipping off the coast — unlike the First World War — and the first recorded incident came as late as December, 1944. It was the bombs and guns of the air raiders and their lethal cargoes of mines which proved the real menace to shipping routes and to the port of Milford Haven, which was a major assembly point for convoys.

The war's first casualty — as in 1914-18 — was not as a result of enemy action, however. The British cargo ship *Mervyn*, on her way from Barry to Lisbon with coal, was in collision with the *Langleeford* and sank 10 miles south-east of the Smalls, on November 1st, 1939. The following January, the Greek steamship *Adamantios J. Pithis* was wrecked at St Ann's Head, as she was nearing the end of a voyage from the Argentinian port of Rosario to Sharpness with a cargo of grain. She was a veteran of the Atlantic run, having been built back in 1918. Angle Lifeboat went to her aid, but a naval patrol vessel had already rescued her master, Captain Glykas, and his crew. One of the first war services of the Tenby Life-boat came on February 3rd, 1940. At just after 1.40 p.m. the coastguards reported that the Norwegian heavy lift ship *Belpareil* was in need of assistance.

A strong south-easterly wind was sweeping across the seaside town as the lifeboat left her station twenty minutes later. Visibility was bad, but the *Belpareil* was found fast on rocks in Drinkem Bay, Caldey Island. The captain would not let his crew leave the ship and an hour later the lifeboat was back at Tenby. The next day, a Sunday, it was learned that the crew had in fact left the vessel and were sheltering in an old shed on the island and were short of food.

The Norwegian consul at Milford was alerted and on the Monday, the lifeboat took him out to Caldey, together with a doctor and the chief coastguard. Twenty-seven of the *Belpareil*'s crew were brought back to the mainland and after being given a hot meal they were sent to Swansea by the consul. Four men remained on the island, including one who was ill. The *Belpareil* was finally refloated on April 20th and left the island escorted by two tugs. For services to the crew, the ship's owners gave the monastic community on Caldey two of the vessel's boats.

After repairs, the *Belpareil* continued to be employed throughout the war carrying heavy lift cargoes for Britain. She received special mention from General Montgomery when she supplied port equipment and barges for the Eighth Army's advance in North Africa in 1942, and the invasion of Italy the following year.

Off the North Pembrokeshire coast on February 26th, 1940, a shore boat from St David's saved the crew of four of the Dutch motor vessel *Ida*, which sank after hitting a submerged object.

With the fall of France, the first magnetic mine attack on Milford Haven by aircraft came early in July, 1940. And a few days before the destruction of the *Thorold* in the August, the Luftwaffe bombed and sunk the trawler *Valeria* off the Smalls.

On October 10th, the Angle Lifeboat was launched after red flares were seen north-west of Skokholm Island at about five o'clock in the morning. Three miles north-west of St Ann's Head, the lifeboat found four members of the crew of the *Alderney Queen*, a London-registered motor vessel. The little ship had been bombed and machine-gunned by enemy aircraft and went down off Grassholm Island. The four survivors transferred from their boat to the lifeboat, which landed them at Milford Haven. The other six members of the *Alderney Queen*'s crew were believed to have been rescued by another vessel.

One of the great mysteries of the war was the disappearance the following month of the Irish Channel cargo steamship *Ardmore*. She was built as the *Killiney* in 1918 for the Dublin-Liverpool service, but before her completion she was transferred to the fleet of the British and Irish Steam Packet Company. The prefix 'Lady' was added to her name, but in 1923, when she was sold to the City of Cork Steam Packet Company, she again became the plain *Ardmore*. For many years she sailed on the Cork-Liverpool service, although in 1940 she was operating on the Rosslare-Fishguard Harbour route. She left Cork for the North Pembrokeshire port on November 11th, but nothing more was heard of her or her crew until the body of the master, Captain T. Ford, was washed up some days later. There were no survivors and it was presumed that the ship had been sunk by enemy action.

At Milford Haven, meanwhile, there was a round-the-clock operation to sweep the port's main channel clear of mines. Acoustic, as well as magnetic mines, were being dropped into the Haven and during the second-half of 1940 just two trawlers were available for minesweeping duties — the *Courtier* and the *Georgette*.

A 40-foot motor boat was the first known victim to an acoustic mine at the port. Then, on November 21st, 1940, the 6,426 ton merchant ship *Dakotian* sank in Dale Roads

The merchant ship 'Dakotian', which sank in Dale Roads, Milford Haven, in November, 1940 – a victim of magnetic mines laid by the Luftwaffe.

(Picture: Real Photographs).

after a number of magnetic mines fell around her. Built in 1922 for the Leyland Line of Liverpool, she was bought by Donaldson Bros in 1934, and was sailing under that company's flag when war broke out. When she arrived in the Haven that black November, she was carrying a general cargo and tinplate. The bow of the vessel was 'dispersed' because it was a navigational hazard but for many years the ship slumbered on the sea bed largely intact and just 10 feet below the surface at low tide. Among the relics brought up from the ship during salvage operations in 1976 was a four-inch Vickers gun of 1918 vintage.

The day after the *Dakotian* incident, the 3,683 ton Ropner steamship *Pikepool* struck a mine a few miles off Linney Head and sank with the loss of six of her officers and eleven men. Her captain, J. B. Atkinson, and other survivors spent 48 hours adrift on water-logged rafts before being rescued.

The Luftwaffe chalked up further successes on November 24th at Milford Haven, when mines claimed the 630 ton salvage vessel *Preserver* and the big steamship *Behar*. The little salvage ship went down near the port's number one buoy, and the *Behar* was towed into shallow water off Great Castle Head where she eventually broke up.

An early war loss for the Holland-America Line was their 19-year old ship *Beemsterdyk*, which left Glasgow in ballast for Cardiff on January 24th, 1941. Two days out, she struck a mine 12 miles off the Smalls. The explosion ripped through her starboard side and she began to heel over. The captain and crew of forty-one abandoned ship, but as she was still afloat an hour later, the master, two engineers and the radio operator went back on board. Two of her holds were filled with water and her auxiliary engines were flooded. But the captain felt that if the weather held, there was an outside chance of saving the vessel. The rest of the crew returned to the ship, and hoisted the lifeboats.

As daylight broke on January 27th, the wind began to increase. The *Beemsterdyk* started to roll and pitch and heavy seas came over the port side. Soon the stern was submerged and when the bulkhead between the flooded holds collapsed, the order was given to take to the boats. Within two minutes, however, she went under. There was no time to lower the boats or cut the falls and thirty-nine men died with her. Of the four who got away by clinging to a raft, one died before they were picked up by the Dunmore East Lifeboat off the Irish coast four days later.

The Royal Navy lost one of their motor gun boats at Milford Haven on February 3rd, when *MGB 12* was mined. She was one of 35 MGBs built by the British Power Company and only six were war losses.

The St David's Lifeboat was involved in another rescue operation, when on March 3rd the motor vessel *Port Townsville* was bombed and set on fire north of St David's Head. When the lifeboat reached the area, it was found that the captain and crew had got safely away in the ship's boats. The *Port Townsville* sank the following day.

March was a particularly successful month for the Luftwaffe. On the 12th, the Ministry of War Transport's *Empire Frost* was attacked and bombed eight miles off the Smalls. She was taken in tow by other ships in her convoy, but on the 13th, enemy aircraft returned to finish her off. Six men

died in the attacks and her captain, J. McClelland, was among the survivors.

On the 21st, bombers raiding the Bristol Channel commerce routes located and destroyed the steamer *London II*, about 18 miles south-south-east of Caldey Island. Six miles away, they found the little coaster *Millisle* and she too was sent to the bottom, with the loss of nine of her crew and the gunner. There were only three survivors. The following day, a Saturday, an even smaller ship, the 495 ton *St Fintan*, was bombed and sunk seven miles north-west of the Smalls.

The Angle Lifeboat's first major service of 1941 came on March 26th, after coast-guards reported that the cable-laying and repairing ship *Faraday* was on fire 1 1/2 miles

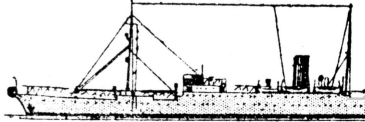

Wartime recognition drawing of the 'Faraday', a cable-laying and repairing ship which sank off St. Ann's Head in March, 1941, after being bombed by the Luftwaffe.

117

off St Ann's Head as a result of an enemy air attack. The lifeboat was launched within an hour and met a Belgian trawler, which had some of the *Faraday*'s crew on board and its boats in tow. A west-south-westerly wind was blowing and the sea was rough so, as the trawler was unable to enter Milford Haven in darkness, the lifeboat escorted her to smooth water. Fifty-six of the survivors were taken off the trawler and landed at Milford. The *Faraday* sank the next day, having lost sixteen of her crew of one hundred and twenty-five. A salvage operation later recovered 90 miles of submarine cable from the wreck.

The last casualty of that month was the steamship *Meg Merrilies*, which was sunk by aircraft near the St Govan's Light Vessel on the 27th. But on April 1st, two large motor vessels, the *San Conrado* and the Norwegian *Hidlefjord*, were bombed and lost off the Smalls. Twenty-nine of the *Hidlefjord*'s crew were killed.

Among the little minesweeping fleet at Milford Haven was the *Johanna Caroline* — one of a number of Dutch trawlers sent to the port for sweeping duties. It was one of

these vessels, the *Rotterdam*, which swept the first acoustic mine in the Haven on February 18th, 1941. The same type of mine was to prove deadly for the *Johanna Caroline*. She was sweeping in about 70 feet of water on April 28th, when there was an explosion directly beneath her. When the smoke had cleared, all that could be seen was wreckage. There were no survivors. Three bodies were recovered, including that of the commanding officer, Lieut. J. van Bueren Lensinck, and these were buried in Milford Haven Cemetery. Among those lost was the legendary 'Uncle' Albert de Graaf, one of the bravest of trawler captains.

Another of the Haven's naval vessels went down on June 7th, when a 280 ton examination ship was mined off the entrance to the port. The previous month, the trawler *Tankerton Towers* was lost near the St Govan's Light Vessel and the motor vessel *Begerin* went down off the South Bishop Lighthouse. Both were victims of Luftwaffe bombers.

In the second week of June, an unsuccessful bid was made to save the British cargo ship, *Baron Carnegie*, after she had been bombed off the coast of North Pembrokeshire. She was on passage, in ballast, with a convoy bound from Swansea to the Gold Coast, when the enemy aircraft attacked. Twenty-five of her crew were killed and damage to the ship was extensive, but an attempt was made to tow her towards Fishguard. Early on the following day, however, she sank off Strumble Head. The St David's Lifeboat had been launched to go to her aid, but found that the survivors had been picked up by other vessels in the vicinity. The lifeboat later landed seven bodies of the ship's crew. Among the survivors was the master, Captain G. S. Cumming. He subsequently took command of the *Baron Erskine* but on New Year's Day, 1942, this ship fell out of convoy in the North Atlantic and was never seen again. It was assumed she had been sunk by a submarine.

The Friday of that second week in June, 1941 — the 13th — proved one of the blackest days in the history of the port of Fishguard. The cross-channel ferry *St Patrick*, had left Rosslare for North Pembrokeshire early that morning, and was about 12 miles from Strumble Head when the German bombers found her. It was no her first encounter with the Luftwaffe. The previous summer she had been attacked on the crossing but had reached port safely. This time there was to be no escape. The first bomb struck her between the bridge and the funnel, penetrating the oil tanks and setting them on fire. When the Fishguard Lifeboat arrived on the scene some hours later, all she found were oil bubbles coming to the surface and two boxes of fish. At this time, it was not known that the ship on fire was the *St Patrick*. But when the Fishguard Lifeboat returned to port later, the boxes of fish were identified as part of the ferry's cargo. The Fishguard Lifeboat searched throughout that morning but found nothing. The St David's Lifeboat and a naval patrol vessel were also involved in the operation. Later, however, news reached the port that the majority of the people on board the *St Patrick* had been rescued and landed at Milford Haven. Seventeen of her crew, a gunner and twelve passengers were lost — the ferry having sunk within five minutes of the attack. Among those who died was the *St Patrick*'s captain, Jim Faraday, and his twenty year old son Jack, a Merchant Navy officer cadet who had decided to accompany his father on that fateful trip. Jack's two brothers also died in the war — one transferring from the Army to the Royal Air Force, after the sinking of the *St Patrick*, to seek his own revenge on the Luftwaffe. For her bravery in saving women passengers trapped on the lower deck, stewardess Miss Elizabeth May Owen was awarded the George Medal.

Many captains survived the loss of one ship, only to die at sea in another air attack months later. One such master was Captain Alfred Tyrrell, whose command, the *Dudley Rose*, was sunk off Devon's Berry Head in April, 1941. Twelve weeks later he and seven of his crew were killed when the *Fowey Rose* was bombed and sunk twenty miles southwest of St Govan's Head. On July 6th, the trawler *Westfield* was lost by enemy action, also off St Govan's Head. In separate incidents in September, the steamship *Empire Gunner* and the motor vessel *Daru* were bombed and sunk off the North Pembrokeshire coast.

Towards the early summer of 1941, the Luftwaffe eased up on their mine-laying attacks on Milford Haven. But in July, 1942, there was a three-night onslaught. Forty-two mines were laid and it was the only

Wartime recognition drawing of the cross-channel ferry 'St. Patrick', bombed and sunk 12 miles off Strumble Head in June, 1941.

occasion throughout the war that the port was closed to sea traffic for more than a few hours. When the little Dutch fleet of mine-sweepers lost another vessel in January, 1942 it was the result, not of a mine, but of a collision off the port. The casualty was the trawler *Eveline* which went down on the 27th. The only other ship to be lost in Pembrokeshire waters that year was the motor vessel *Empire Beacon*, which sank off St Ann's Head on April 5th. She was the third '*Empire*' ship to go down off the coast during the war. A fourth, the *Empire Panther*, sank on New Year's Day, 1943, after hitting a mine eight miles off Strumble Head on a voyage from New York to Cardiff. Six of her crew were killed.

In March 1943, at Milford Haven, the port mourned the loss of the trawler *Moray*, which was in use as a victualling store ship. The vessel, which foundered off the Haven, had been built in 1918 and for the early part of the Second World War was hired by the Admiralty as a danlayer.

The year proved a hectic one for the Angle and St David's Lifeboats. In April, the St David's boat had been involved in that

The oil tanker 'Athelduchess' which broke in two after running on to rocks near the Smalls lighthouse in August, 1943.

difficult service when two landing craft were lost. Late on August 20th, coastguards reported a ship ashore inside the south-east rocks of the Smalls. The tanker *Athelduchess*, of Liverpool, had been in convoy from Swansea to New York in ballast when she stranded on the rocks near the Smalls lighthouse in a fresh wind and rough sea. News of her plight reached the St David's lifeboat station at 12.30 in the morning, and the Angle station 25 minutes later.

Both lifeboats were launched and at 1.30 a.m. the St David's boat was told by radio that the tanker's crew of over sixty were abandoning ship. It was reported that ship's boats were drifting in a north-easterly direction and at 3 a.m. the lifeboat found one of the boats and rescued its four occupants. She then made for the tanker, which was still upright on the rocks, with ladders in position on her sides. The captain had evidently decided that it was not necessary for more members of the crew to leave the ship. One of the tanker's boats had already left the vicinity.

Two tugs were now standing by the *Athelduchess* and as the Angle Lifeboat was on its way, the St David's Lifeboat left to search for the other ship's boat. This was located at 4.30 a.m. and five men were rescued. The St David's Lifeboat went back to the tanker and stood by until daylight, when she returned to her station with the rescued crewmen. The survivors were given clothes and food and were later picked up by transport from the Milford Haven naval base.

The Angle Lifeboat reached the wreck at 4.15 a.m. after ploughing 22 miles through rough seas. She found the tugs were waiting for high water before attempting to haul the tanker off the rocks and the lifeboat helped to pass hawsers in preparation for the operation. When high water came, however, the tugs failed to move the ship and her captain decided he now had no alternative but to abandon her. The Angle Lifeboat took off the fifty-six men still on board and later transferred some of them to a salvage vessel. The remainder were landed at Milford Haven before the Angle boat returned to her station after being out on service for 17 hours.

The *Athelduchess* subsequently broke in two on the rocks. The after part was successfully taken in tow and beached at Dale, and although the forward part had taken the ground it refloated and drifted out to sea before sinking. In 1948, a new-look *Athelduchess* returned to sea with a new fore part and the greater part of her midship section also new. She was reclassed as the *Milford*, and sailed under the Norwegian flag for some years. In 1954, she was sold to Antwerp interests for use as an oil depot at the Belgian port.

Coxswain James Watkins, of the Angle Lifeboat, was sixty-seven when, in December 1943, he and his crew performed one of the outstanding rescues of the war. Early on the evening of the 18th, a small Dutch coaster, the *Thor*, was running for shelter in a south-westerly gale when she was overwhelmed by a following sea off St Ann's Head. The ship was thrown on her beam ends and when the lifeboat reached her, searchlights revealed the coaster awash, with heavy seas breaking over her. She looked, Coxswain Watkins reported later, 'like a half-tide rock'. A tug was standing by, but could do nothing, and although it was dangerous for the lifeboat to go any closer Coxswain Watkins made the bid. Some of the *Thor*'s crew had abandoned ship and were in the water. It was pitch dark and they were difficult to see, but the lifeboat picked up two of them. A third was carried away and was drowned.

Coxswain Watkins then took the lifeboat to the leeward side of the wreck, which was nearly bottom up. Gear and wreckage made the approach hazardous, but he brought the lifeboat so close to the ship that his crew were able to drag two of the seamen to safety with veering lines. Two more survivors were able to jump into the lifeboat from the bottom of the *Thor*. There was now no-one left on board the wreck. Six of her crew of ten had been saved by the lifeboat, one had been rescued by the tug and three were lost.

Coxswain Watkins's gallantry was recognised with the award of the silver medal of the Royal National Lifeboat Institution. He had handled the lifeboat with great skill and daring and his responsibility and risks were increased as he did not have all his regular crew with him. The lifeboat's motor mechanic, Albert E. Rees, was awarded the Thanks of the Institution on Vellum.

When James Watkins retired in 1946, he had served 24 years as coxswain of Angle Lifeboat, 13 years as second coxswain, and had been awarded the R.N.L.I.'s silver medal, the bronze medal for the *Molesey* rescue in 1929, and a clasp to his bronze award. This second bronze came after another gallant rescue on July 16th, 1945, when the naval authorities reported that a vessel was ashore on Grassholm Island and was in need of help. It has been blowing hard all night from the west-north-west and there were rough seas with a dangerous ground swell. The Angle Lifeboat was launched soon after noon and she found the ship in distress was the ex-German steamer, *Walter L. M. Russ*, manned by seventeen men from South Shields. The ship was on rocks about 50 yards from the western end of the island and the heavy seas were making a clean sweep over her. Only the bridge, the upper part of the funnel and two masts could be seen above the water. Two men were clinging to the funnel ladder and another was in the main top. Damaged rigging and gear was hanging loose, which made the lifeboat's approach difficult. But Coxswain Watkins succeeded in anchoring to the seaward of the wreck and was able to drop down close enough to fire a line to the ship. As the funnel was in danger of being washed away at any moment, the first line went to the two men on the funnel ladder. Despite exhaustion, the two were able to fix the tackle of the breeches buoy to the funnel and were hauled to safety. Several times a line was fired to the man in the main top before he was able to seize it. He, too, was hauled to the lifeboat. The rescue of all three men had taken two hours. From the survivors it was learned that other members of the crew were on Grassholm Island. A search revealed six of them on rocks, which were being swept by the seas.

It was too dangerous to anchor close to that rocky shore and drop down the cable, so the coxswain took the lifeboat as near as he could six times. On each occasion, a line was thrown out and a man dragged to safety. Eight of the ship's crew were still missing, and a further search failed to find them. The nine survivors were in need of medical attention and the lifeboat headed back to land them at Milford Haven, after over 10 hours at sea.

A few months earlier — on March 28th — Angle Lifeboat went to the aid of a 5,225 ton merchant ship, *Antonio*, which had been damaged in a collision with another cargo vessel, the *Fort Moose*. The lifeboat transferred six of the *Antonio's* survivors from another ship before returning to her station. The *Antonio* remained afloat for three days, finally sinking five miles off St Ann's Head.

Both the Angle and St David's Lifeboats went out on January 9th, 1945, after the American steamer *Jonas Lie* was torpedoed off Grassholm. They were recalled, however, when it was learned that the crew had been rescued by the St Mary's Lifeboat from the Scilly Isles.

Submarines had begun to make their presence felt off the Pembrokeshire coast in the latter half of 1944, as Luftwaffe air bases in France began to fall to the Allies. On December 10th, 1944, the American Liberty Ship, *Dan Beard*, was torpedoed seven miles off Strumble Head by *U-1202*. The after-part of the vessel sank, but the bow section eventually drifted ashore and was wrecked. Distress flares from the ship had been sighted by coastguards late in the afternoon, and the Fishguard Lifeboat was launched at 6 p.m. When she reached the scene, the crippled ship was surrounded by oil and wreckage and there was no one on board. A search began for survivors but the lifeboat found only a ship's lifebuoy with a light. One of the lifeboatmen, T. M. Neal, had now been taken seriously ill and the lifeboat sped back to Fishguard in the rough seas.

Lifeboatman Neal was transferred to a police car at the harbour but shortly after reaching his home he died. Numbed by this incident, the coxswain and crew returned to sea again, at the request of the naval authorities, to continue the search for survivors from the Liberty ship. By daylight, neither boats nor men had been found. The St David's Lifeboat was also taking part in the rescue operation and near Strumble Head found wreckage and oil and then a raft carrying twelve men. Their clothing was saturated in oil and their hands were very greasy and difficulty was experienced in getting them into the lifeboat. Lifeboatman J. Jenkins transferred to the raft to steady it and eventually the twelve survivors were taken on board. One was seriously injured and died before the lifeboat could reach Fishguard.

It was still dark when the lifeboat turned out of Fishguard Harbour to resume the search, but nothing was found. At daybreak, she returned to her station — the hands, arms and faces of her crew black with oil from the stricken ship, and slight damage to her hull from wreckage. The Flag Officer in

125

charge of the naval base at Milford Haven expressed his appreciation for the help given by the lifeboats. It was later revealed that all but twenty-nine of the *Dan Beard*'s crew had been saved.

The Milford Haven base had itself suffered a blow a week earlier when the Admiralty collier *P.L.M. 21* grounded and sank off the port. The *U-1302* — a sister boat to the submarine which had destroyed the *Dan Beard* — began a patrol in the Bristol Channel and Irish Sea in February, 1945, just three months before the end of the war with Germany. One of her first victims was the motor vessel *Norfolk Coast*, which was torpedoed seven miles off the South Bishop on February 28th. Seven of the ship's crew were killed and one of the six wounded died soon after being landed.

On March 2nd, the U-boat sank the *King Edgar*, a 5,536 tons motor vessel, 20 miles north-west of St David's Head. Time, however, was running out for the submarine. Five days later, she was caught in the vicinity by three Royal Canadian Navy frigates, the *La Hulloise*, *Strathadam* and *Thetford Mines*, and depth-charged to destruction.

Early that summer, another U-boat moved up the waters of Milford Haven towards Pembroke Dock. But with the war against Germany already won, *U-861* was merely on its way to go on show at the dockyard town, which had suffered so much at the hands of the Luftwaffe.

Wartime recognition drawing of the Norwegian heavy lift ship 'Belpareil', which ran on to rocks at Caldey Island in February, 1940.

The South Coast

Robert Honyman, Captain of His Majesty's late ship *Leda*, shivered involuntarily as he entered the great cabin of the *Salvador del Mundo*. The weak March sunshine filtered in through the stern windows, catching the gold braid of the semi-circle of officers who had sat in judgment at his court martial. But Honyman saw only his sword on the table in front of the president's seat. Its hilt was towards him — he was not guilty. It was five weeks since his frigate had been wrecked, but it seemed like yesterday . . . the howling wind, the mountainous seas, the terrible crash as the ship struck the rocks.

H.M.S. Leda, of 38 guns, had been on patrol in the Irish Sea protecting the trade routes from French privateers. She had left Cork on January 25th, 1808, on the orders of Vice-Admiral Whitshed, but the following day, she ran into a heavy gale and was forced to reduce sail. The frigate shipped tremendous seas, which broke the boats from their lashings and turned them keel upwards on the deck. The after gunroom was flooded with six or eight inches of water and some of the provisions had been damaged.

Honyman decided that he had no alternative but to seek shelter and he made for Milford Haven. At 5.30 p.m. on Sunday, January 31st, the ship was off St Ann's Head and James Garretty, a pilot who had joined the frigate at Cork, prepared to take her in to an anchorage inside the Haven. He had piloted the gun brig *H.M.S. Virago* into the harbour the previous week and asked that a special look out be kept for Stack Rock, well up the Haven off South Hook Point. When a rock was sighted ahead, the pilot praised the man who had reported it and begged that it be given a wide berth to starboard. In fact the rock was Thorn Island, just inside the entrance to the port and by taking a course to starboard the frigate ran on to rocks at West Angle Bay.

It was shortly before high water, and in an effort to haul the ship off Honyman ordered a stream anchor to be carried out and the cable was hove taut. But the frigate was stuck fast. Honyman was later advised by the quarantine master at Milford that as the gale was increasing there was a great risk of the ship breaking up. The masts were cut away and the *Leda*'s company were taken ashore early the following morning.

At low water, the weather moderated and further attempts were made to haul the frigate off, again without success. The guns were thrown overboard and the task of removing stores and provisions began. *H.M.S. Leda* became a total loss, although timbers and fittings from the ship were used in the construction of another 38-gun frigate, *H.M.S. Surprise*, laid down in 1808 at Milford and launched four years later. Honyman, his officers and crew, and the pilot, James Garretty, appeared at the court martial on board *H.M.S. Salvador del Mundo* at Plymouth on March 3rd, 1808, and were severally acquitted.

The court martial found that the loss of the *Leda* was as a result of the pilot mistaking Thorn Island for Stack Rock. The pilot had 'acted to the best of his judgement' and no blame was attached to Captain Honyman, his officers or crew, or to the pilot, for the loss of the ship.

Over a century later, the Haven was stunned by one of the worst fishing vessel disasters on that stretch of the coastline. The Lowestoft drifter *Shore Breeze* struck the rocks off St Ann's Head in a heavy squall on January 5th, 1936. Coastguards joined members of the Life-Saving Apparatus Company in a rescue bid and made their way along the cliffs in a 90 m.p.h. gale. There were times when they could only crawl on their hands and knees; and, when they reached the area where the drifter was reported in distress, there was no trace of her or her crew. She had gone down within minutes taking all ten fishermen to their deaths — or so it was thought.

A week later, an Angle fisherman, Sidney Hicks, was passing the Head in his motor boat when he noticed human legs jutting over a ledge high up on the cliffs. He alerted the coastguards and two men were lowered down to the ledge, which was a hundred feet above the sea. There, in a sitting position, was the body of one of the crew of the ill-fated drifter. He was only partly clothed, his left hand was gripping the rocks, his mouth was wide open and his eyes looked upwards. His legs from the knees down were severely bruised and bloodstained — he had cheated death in the wreck and made a wild climb for life. An overhanging rock had trapped him on the ledge, and he had died from exposure just thirty feet from safety.

The entrance to Milford Haven became the graveyard for many ships racing for shelter. The schooner *George and Francis* was lost at West Angle Bay on January 14th, 1852, after running onto rocks. Another schooner, the *Breeze*, foundered off St Ann's Head on November 25th, 1875, when she sprung a leak. As recently as 1964, a Royal Navy boom defence vessel, *Barking*, was wrecked at Mill Bay. She was under tow to Swansea to be scrapped when the line parted in a gale and she drifted into the bay. One of the last services of the Angle Lifeboat *Katherine* — first lifeboat on the station which was opened in 1868 — was to the Wexford schooner *Slaney*, which was dragging her anchors in Dale Roads on September 26th, 1883. Three of the crew were taken off by the lifeboat when the *Slaney*'s cables parted soon afterwards. She drove onto rocks and quickly broke up. The schooner's captain and mate were rescued from the shore.

As early as 1833 the silver medal of the Royal National Institution for the Preservation of Life from Shipwreck was awarded to William Field for a rescue in the Haven. The Sicilian brig *Felicita* was wrecked at Sandy Haven Bay and Field swam through the surf to save twelve people. A silver medal also went to Thomas Landells in 1850 for rescuing the crew of eight from the schooner *Maria* at Pill Point.

Dale Roads afforded shelter 'from all but easterly winds'. The veteran topsail schooner *Ethel May*, of Chester, came to

The schooner 'Ethel May', of Chester, wrecked in Dale Roads in January, 1936.

(Picture: National Maritime Museum).

grief there on January 6th, 1936, after 58 years of trading. Her crew was saved by the rocket apparatus. The following month, the topsail schooner *Nellie Fleming* vanished in a south-easterly gale off the South Pembrokeshire coast. She was on passage from Lydney to Youghal and wreckage, believed to have come from the ship, was later found off

The three-masted topsail schooner 'Nellie Fleming', which disappeared in a gale off the South Pembrokeshire coast in February, 1936. (Picture: National Maritime Museum).

The Israeli cargo ship 'Etrog' on fire off the Pembrokeshire coast in June, 1961. Alongside her is one of Milford Haven's fire-fighting tugs and the former Tenby Life-Boat 'John R. Webb', on temporary duty at Angle. (Picture: Harold Rees).

The ketch 'Progress' which ended her days at Angle, after being beached there in 1954.   (Picture: National Maritime Museum).

The last remains of the ketch 'Progress' at Angle Bay.

(Picture: Martin Cavaney).

Milford Haven. It was to Dale Roads that the Israeli cargo ship *Etrog* was brought after being damaged by fire in June, 1961, 13 miles off the Smalls. The ship was given permission to enter the port and was escorted in by the Angle Lifeboat, which had taken off some of the passengers and wives and children of the ship's officers. The fire-fighting tugs *Thorngarth* and *Anglegarth* beached the ship at Dale and a hole was cut in her plating to flood the burning hold.

In October, 1949, the crippled British steamer *Cydonia* was towed into the Haven and beached at East Angle Bay. She had hit a mine 30 miles north of Strumble Head. Five years later, in the great storm of November, 1954, the coaster *Ability* was blown onto rocks at Scotch Bay, Milford Haven. The Angle Lifeboat stood by the ship, as the crew were saved from the shore.

As the days of sail had come virtually to an end, the little creeks and bays of the Haven all too often became the site of abandoned trading ships, which rotted away until only their skeletons remained. The hulk of the *Bertha Grace* lay for many years on a beach at Pembroke Dock and on the opposite shore,

The remains of the coastal trader 'Mary Jane Lewis' at Angle. She was built at Pennar's Jacobs Pill yard at Pembroke Dock, and is one of several 'skeletons' of vessels on the shores of the Milford Haven waterway.

(Picture: Martin Cavaney).

at Neyland, are the remains of the brigantine *Sela*, built at Prince Edward Island, Nova Scotia, in 1859. Another Atlantic veteran, the *Rosie*, built at Appledore in 1885 as a schooner and refitted as an auxiliary ketch in 1912, also ended her days at Milford Haven. For eighteen years, she sailed twice a year across the Atlantic and traded along the Labrador coast. The ketch *Progress*, of Bideford, sailed regularly to Newfoundland and her few remaining timbers are at East Angle Bay, with the skeletons of four other vessels, including the *Mary Jane Lewis*, which was built at Pembroke Dock.

The *Progress* was towed into Milford Haven in June, 1954, for repairs, after she had taken in water and developed engine trouble. She resumed her voyage to the Canary Islands in the July, but was again hit by engine trouble and was towed back to Angle, where she remained. Some of her fittings were saved and are on display at the National Maritime Museum.

One of Pembrokeshire's most beautiful beaches — Freshwater West — is also one of the most dangerous, with great seas rolling in, unchecked, from the Atlantic. The owner and crew of the schooner, *Wave*, of Aberystwyth, perished there when the vessel was wrecked on October 26th, 1859. And in 1861, John Large was awarded the R.N.L.I.'s silver medal for assisting in the resuce of the crew of three of the brig *Harmony* on February 19th. Large had waded into the treacherous surf at Freshwater West to reach the survivors. The following year, 1862, a Pembroke man named Young was presented with a bravery medal for saving the crew of a French ship which foundered on the sands. Over a century later, the medal was sold at auction for £52.

The Angle Lifeboat, the *Henry Dundas*, brought the tug *Wrestler* into Milford Haven in April, 1927, after successfully re-floating her from Freshwater West. When the lifeboat reached the scene, the crew of the tug had already taken to a boat, but it capsized in the surf and the Master and Chief Engineer were drowned. Lifeboatmen boarded the tug, made temporary repairs, and with the help of other vessels got the *Wrestler* off the rocks.

South of Freshwater West is the great

bulk of Linney Head, which has witnessed the deaths of hundreds of seamen. Offshore are the Crow and Toes rocks, with the Brimstone Rocks also taking a share in the wrecking. It was off Linney Head in 1797 that a small yacht owned by Lord Cawdor foundered, after being stolen by French prisoners. They had been captured during the abortive invasion at Fishguard and were imprisoned at Pembroke. But two local women smuggled digging implements to them and they tunnelled their way to freedom. The women fled with them and the yacht was cast adrift after the prisoners captured a coastal brig off Linney.

The brigantine *Dispatch*, on passage from Nova Scotia to the West Country, was disabled in a gale in December, 1848, and was blown on to rocks at Linney. Her crew took to the ship's boat, but when they attempted to land at Freshwater West, the craft was swamped in the breakers and there was only one survivor. Many of those who died off Linney were buried in the churchyards of the coastal parishes. At Castlemartin is the grave of David Davies, of Aberystwyth, lost on the headland on the night of April 23rd, 1857, in the schooner *Robert and Mary*.

The burial register also listed the passengers and crew of the *Edinburgh*, wrecked on Linney on February 8th, 1839, on a voyage from New Orleans to Liverpool. The crew of the Liverpool steamship *Amelia*, were saved by Angle Lifeboat on October 28th, 1874, after the vessel was ripped open by Crow Rock. The Bridgwater trading ketch, *Florrie*, ended her useful life on the same rock on July 3rd, 1918. The little 94-ton ship was a familiar visitor to ports throughout Britain and Europe, and was wrecked twenty-six years after her launching. When the steamer *Princess Irene* broke her back on the Brimstone Rocks in 1907, she ran almost on top of the wreck of another steamer, the *Humber*.

One of the great wreck puzzles of Linney was the disappearance of the former British motor ferry *Balholm* in January, 1979. The 240-ton vessel, en route to Ireland, developed engine trouble off South Pembrokeshire and drifted towards Crow Rock on January 21st. Angle Lifeboat found the ship in a perilous position, and Coxswain Rees Holmes took the lifeboat

The former motor ferry 'Balholm' which disappeared off Linney Head in January, 1979.   (Picture: Western Telegraph).

alongside in a heavy swell, with winds of force five to six. The *Balholm*'s skipper, Paul Webb, and the three men, two women and a youth on board the ship, refused help and the vessel subsequently dropped two anchors about half-a-mile west of Crow Rock. Later, however, Webb and his crew agreed to be taken off by the lifeboat. The ship remained at anchor for some days, but by the morning of January 26th, she had vanished and it was presumed she had sunk at her moorings in moderate seas in less than 60 feet of water. On February 2nd, a life-jacket marked 'Balholm' was found on Lydstep Beach, 15 miles to the east, and three weeks later, a lifeboat and several life-jackets, also marked with her name, were picked up by a Milford trawler 43 miles west-north-west of Linney Head. But the case of her sinking remains a mystery.

One of the major rescue operations off South Pembrokeshire since the Second World War centred on Flimstone Head, between Linney and St Govan's. Early on March 27th, 1946, the Greek cargo ship *Nicolaou Virginia*, bound from the South American port of Bahia Blanca to Glasgow, ran ashore in thick fog. The ship was badly damaged and her S.O.S. was picked up by Land's End Radio and passed to Tenby Coastguard. Tenby's Lifeboat, the *John R. Webb*, was launched at four in the morning and stood by the vessel, with a tug and a salvage steamer.

That evening, three of the crew, who had been picked up from a boat, were put ashore at Broad Haven, several miles away. The Tenby Lifeboat then returned to the ship and remained with her throughout the night. The next morning, it was decided to call out the Angle Lifeboat, the *Elizabeth Elson*, to relieve the Tenby boat, which returned to her station taking three more of the Greek steamer's crew with her. The *John R. Webb* had been on service for over thirty-four hours.

The Angle boat stood by all day and at nine that night transferred twenty-six of the ship's crew to the salvage steamer. Only four men were now on board the *Nicolaou Virginia*, but they were also taken off five hours later when the Angle Lifeboat headed for home, having been at sea for twenty-two hours. Later that day, March 29th, the salvage operations were abandoned and the ship became a total wreck.

One of the few ships to be salvaged from the coast around Flimstone was the steamer *Netherholme*. She was on a voyage, in ballast, from Maryport to Cardiff on November 3rd, 1907, when she ran onto rocks near the Pen-y-Holt Stack. Captain V. Lauder and his crew of fourteen were able to leave the ship at low tide and scaled the cliffs with a rope left behind from salvage operations on the steamer *Shamrock* the previous year. A week later, the *Netherholme* was re-floated and beached at Scotch Bay, Milford Haven. She underwent an examination in dry dock, but in March 1908, it was decided she should be scrapped.

The only lightship to have been stationed off Pembrokeshire marks shoals three miles off St Govan's Head. Over the years, the Tenby and Angle Lifeboats have rendered useful services to the vessels and their crews, but the most dramatic came in September, 1953, when the Tenby boat rescued the lightship's crew of seven.

The lightship was in danger of sinking. Huge seas broke over her and the lifeboat during the rescue operation. At one stage, the lightship rolled onto the lifeboat, but in a brilliant service, Coxswain Thomas 'Josh' Richards took the seven men off in fifteen minutes. Coxswain Richards later received the R.N.L.I.'s silver medal for gallantry and Bowman William Thomas and Motor Mechanic William Rogers were awarded bronze medals. The other lifeboatmen received the Thanks of the Institution on Vellum. The lightship remained afloat and on station, despite having shipped terrific seas, and she was later boarded by members of the Trinity House vessel *Alert*.

One of the earliest recorded wrecks on St Govan's Head was in September, 1835, when the Cardiff brig *Neptune*, went aground with the loss of all but one of her crew. In the 1890s, Coastguard George Calder received the Board of Trade's silver medal for descending the cliffs at St Govan's and bringing up two survivors from the *Annie Park*. The 2,211-ton British cargo ship *Mareca* was wrecked west of the Head on January 21st, 1898, en route from Cork to Newport, in ballast. All on board were saved. One of the worst small boat disasters

The Tenby Life-Boat 'Annie Collin', pictured on the beach below the resort's Castle Hill. She served at Tenby from 1885-1901 and was launched on service 14 times, saving 13 lives.

(Picture: R.N.L.I.).

on this part of the coast was in 1952, when four members of a family of six were drowned. The 48-foot cabin cruiser *Enchantress* ran onto rocks near St Govan's in darkness on August 17th and the heavy seas soon smashed her to pieces. The first hint of the tragedy came when one of the two survivors, twelve year old Anthony Sweeney, knocked at the door of a caravan close to the village of Bosherston some miles away and begged for help. He was in a state of collapse, but was able to reveal the details of that tragic night. His father, a fifty year old Birmingham businessman, his mother and his two sisters, aged sixteen and nine, had all perished.

There has been a lifeboat at Tenby since 1852, but as far back as 1835 a silver medal for bravery was won by a local man, John Ray, who rescued six people from the schooner *Hunter*, with a shore boat. In 1855, the R.N.L.I.'s silver medal was awarded to Lieutenant Richard Jesse, Chief Officer of Coastguard. He was in command of the lifeboat which saved the crews of the schooners *Agenoria*, of Bideford, and *Alexandra*, of Le Havre, on December 18th of that year.

Lieutenant Jesse's medal is now on display at the Lifeboat Museum at R.N.L.I. Headquarters in Poole, Dorset.

Robert Parrott, Chief Boatman of Tenby Coastguard, was voted the Institution's silver medal in recognition of his repeated services in saving life from shipwreck. He gained a second silver award in 1859 after a rescue operation on November 6th, when the Sunderland brig *Policy* was wrecked at Monkstone Point during a gale. Lieut. R. F. Boyle, R.N. also won a silver medal for this resuce. While in the act of saving the brig's crew, the lifeboat's cable parted and she was forced to return to the shore. The coxswain and crew then made their way across the sands and rocks with the rocket apparatus and brought the survivors safely off the wreck.

In those early years, the lifeboat had to be launched over the beach by a large number of helpers. But when the numbers increased to ninety-seven and one hundred-and-six, on occasions, the R.N.L.I. ordered an investigation. A head launcher was appointed in 1897 to hand out bronze tallies to helpers. The tallies could later be exchanged

Board of Trade 'Rocket Apparatus Company' tokens distributed by its officers among those seen to have volunteered valuable assistance in rescue operations at the scene of a wrecking. These brass tokens (about the size of a 5p coin) were then presented for claim of payment at the nearest H.M. Coastguard Headquarters. (Quadrant).

for helpers' fees. The maximum number of helpers for services was limited to fifty and for exercises to forty, but when a new lifeboat house and slipway was built in 1905, the number of helpers was cut to four.

Many of Tenby Lifeboat's services have been to ships in distress in Caldey Roads. During the darkness of August 21st/22nd, 1868, no fewer than three vessels were wrecked when the wind suddenly changed direction. The crews were picked up by the schooner *Emily Ann*, but she began to drag her anchors and the lifeboat took off her 13 men. The same day, the crew of seven of the Cork ship, *Nameless*, were rescued.

The Tenby station was served by pulling and sailing lifeboats right up to 1923. The last of these was the *William and Mary Devey*, which was launched forty-six times on service in twenty-one years, and saved seventy-nine lives.

One of her final services at Tenby was to the Russian schooner *Tevija*, drifting helplessly off the coast on February 26th, 1923. The ship had been swamped by heavy seas and was almost a total wreck, when the lifeboat battled out to her in the strong south-westerly gale and snatched the crew of eight and a woman passenger to safety.

John H. Williams who served as coxswain of Tenby Life-Boat from 1912-1931. During this period Tenby's last pulling and sailing life-boat, the 'William and Mary Devey', was replaced by the station's first motor life-boat, the 'John R. Webb'. (Picture: R.N.L.I.).

The *William and Mary Devey* was replaced by the station's first motor lifeboat, the *John R. Webb*, which saved thirty-two lives on sixteen services up to 1930. She was succeeded by another *John R. Webb* — the lifeboat of *Fermanagh* fame.

One of this boat's first post-war services involved the cargo ship *Juta*, of the Ministry of War Transport's fleet. She was on a voyage, in ballast, from Rouen to Glasgow, when she was holed off St Govan's Head and sank two miles off Caldey Island. Distress signals were sent out shortly before five in the morning of October 7th, 1945 and when the lifeboat reached her position, she had already gone down. The *Juta*'s crew of twenty were rescued by the minesweeping trawler, *H.M.S. Larch*, and were transferred to the lifeboat, which brought them into Tenby.

The growth of Tenby's tourist industry since the war is reflected in many of the lifeboat's services — offshore and inshore. One such rescue was on September 10th, 1961, when the sailing boat *Iliad* was disabled in a squall and was drifting towards the rocks of Monkstone Point. The *Iliad*'s crew of three clambered onto rocks and then swam the 20 yards to the lifeboat, which was unable to go in any closer because of the depth of water and heavy surf. The sailing boat was wrecked. The rescue attracted particular interest among the many holidaymakers at the resort — but this was no new phenomenon. The Rev. L. East recorded the wreck of the brig *Richard* while on holiday in the town in 1844, and gave a vivid description of the rescue of survivors by Manby's mortar apparatus.

There were few tourists in the town in the great storm of October, 1896, however, when a number of ships were damaged in the resort's little harbour as heavy seas caused chaos in the tightly-packed anchorage. Sixty years earlier, the sloop *Wheatsheaf* was wrecked at Saundersfoot Harbour in another October storm, which breached the harbour's south pier in several places.

The Tenby artist Charles Norris (1779-1858) was fascinated by the sea and ships, which he sketched in fair weather and in storms. When the timber barque *Dorchester* was beached and broken up in 1829 at Tenby, after stranding near Ragwen Point,

144

Pendine, he sketched her at every stage of demolition. A watercolour of the barque is among the extensive Norris collection at Tenby Museum. The collection also includes his illustrations of the collier brig *Durham* wrecked at Saundersfoot on February 23rd, 1839, and the *Nightingale* 'being deserted by her crew in the breakers at Lydstep Bay'.

Tankers in Distress

Cathedral organist Dr Joseph Soar awoke to the incessant ring of the telephone as the storm howled through the still-darkened streets of the little city of St David's. It was a few minutes before six on that cold Saturday morning — November 27th, 1954 — as Dr Soar, lifeboat honorary secretary, hurried to answer the call. A Liberian oil tanker was in distress off the Pembrokeshire coast and the aircraft carrier *H.M.S. Illustrious* was heading to her aid. The 20,125 ton tanker *World Concord*, on a voyage in ballast from Liverpool to Syria, had met hurricane-like conditions in the Irish Sea. One of the worst storms in living memory quickly took its toll on the labouring oil giant.

The tanker broke in two, stranding the master, Captain Athanassiou, and six of the crew on the forward part, and thirty-five men on the aft section which was still being driven along by the unmanned engines. The news that the tanker was broken reached Dr Soar at 6.30 a.m. and anticipating that lifeboats would be needed, the crew of the St David's Boat, *Swn-y-môr*, was assembled. When the signal came the lifeboat was ready to launch, and by 8.30 a.m. she was heading across Ramsey Sound to risks unknown. At 9.15 a.m., *H.M.S. Illustrious* signalled the lifeboat, giving the *World Concord*'s position as 15 miles north-north-west of the South Bishop Lighthouse. The lifeboat butted through the heavy seas, lashed by fierce rain squalls which reduced visibility to about one mile. Shortly after 11.30 a.m., however, the lifeboat coxswain, William Watts Williams, and his crew had the tanker in view — or at least the after part of the ship. The fore part was drifting towards the Irish coast. By now, a fresh gale was blowing from the south with waves reaching 15 to 20 feet in height, and there was a long and powerful swell. When the lifeboat was in the trough of a wave her crew could not see the tanker's masts, and on board the *Illustrious* the lifeboat was only regularly in view on the radar screen.

Coxswain Watts Williams decided to take the lifeboat in on a dummy run to the starboard side of the tanker first. After making the run, he realised that it was

The St. David's Life-Boat 'Swn-y-Mor' alongside the after part of the tanker 'World Concord', which broke in two in hurricane-like conditions in November, 1954.

(Picture: Associated Press).

Coxswain William Watts Williams, of the St. David's Life-Boat, who was awarded the R.N.L.I. silver medal for the rescue of 35 of the crew of the oil tanker 'World Concord' in November, 1954. Coxswain Watts Williams was voted the R.N.L.I.'s bronze medal in 1943 for his devotion to duty in the wartime service to the landing craft, 'LCGs 15' and '16'. (Picture: R.N.L.I.).

essential for the Jacobs ladder on the tanker to be moved away from the stern and the ship's churning propellers. Of those on board, thirty-four were Greek and one was Egyptian, and none could speak English. But, the coxswain made his wishes clear and the Jacobs ladder was re-rigged. He now stationed five men forward in the lifeboat and went in to take off the first of the survivors. The operation was completed successfully and the lifeboat went slowly ahead and then astern — repeating the manoeuvre thirty-four times until all those on the tanker had been taken off.

At 12.30 p.m., the lifeboat left the vicinity and headed, through heavy seas, back to her station. She reached the slipway two-and-a-half hours later, but conditions were such that rehousing the boat proved difficult. However, the survivors were landed safely fifteen minutes later — the lifeboat having been at sea for nearly eight hours.

The shipwrecked seamen were taken to the Royal Naval Air Station at Brawdy, which was playing a vital role in the rescue operations. Naval helicopters had been scrambled in nightmare weather conditions and had reached the fore part of the *World Concord*. But it was not possible to take the captain and six crew members off — even if they had wanted to leave.

By 2 p.m., the gale was approaching hurricane force with winds of 70 to 80 m.p.h. The famous rescue tug *Turmoil* was in the area and *H.M.S. Illustrious* had been joined by the frigate *H.M.S. Orwell*. The Fishguard Lifeboat, which earlier that day had saved the crew of the German coaster *Gramsbergen*, was also ready to launch if required. The fore part of the tanker was then 28 miles south-east of Rosslare, and at 3.30 p.m. the Rosslare Lifeboat was launched. She reached the *World Concord* shortly after 7 p.m., but because of the risk of taking the seven men off in darkness, Coxswain Richard Walsh decided to wait until dawn.

The lifeboat stood by for twelve hours in terrible seas and followed the tanker, which was drifting northwards at about three-and-a-half-knots. Finally, at 8.45 a.m. on the Sunday and after two dummy runs, the Rosslare boat took off all seven men in a brilliant and courageous operation. The survivors were landed at Holyhead at 3.30 p.m., some twenty-six hours after the lifeboat had left Rosslare.

Tugs subsequently took the two sections of the stricken tanker in tow. Exactly a year later, the *World Concord* steamed down the Irish Sea from the Clyde — her two errant sections united by an extra part amidships.

Coxswain Watts Williams and Coxswain Richard Walsh were awarded R.N.L.I. silver medals for their gallantry. Bronze medals went to motor mechanic George Jordan and assistant motor mechanic Gwilym Davies, of St David's, and second coxswain William Duggan and motor mechanic Richard Hickey, of Rosslare. The Thanks of the Institution on Vellum were awarded to second coxswain Dai Lewis, acting bowman William Rowlands and lifeboatmen William Morris, Howell Roberts and Richard Chisholm, of St David's, and to the other members of the Rosslare Lifeboat's crew.

At that time, Milford Haven had yet to be developed as a major oil port. But when six years later the first oil tanker arrived at the port's new Esso refinery terminal, she did so in a blaze of publicity. The occasion, though, was to end in tragedy. When the tanker, the *Esso Portsmouth*, left the Haven she was a blackened hulk — wrecked by explosions and under tow to the Tyne for repairs.

The *Esso Portsmouth* berthed at the refinery terminal on Friday, July 8th, 1960, with 32,000 tons of crude oil from Kuwait. Milford Haven was fast becoming Europe's second biggest oil port. At 6.30 on the Saturday morning, the port was rocked by three violent explosions as the tanker burst into flames. The Haven village of Angle was startled awake by the noise and within eighteen minutes, the local lifeboat had been launched. A huge cloud of black smoke drifted across the Haven and, at one stage, it was thought that three of the tanker's crew were missing. Angle Lifeboat searched the area, without finding anyone, and then

The oil tanker 'Esso Portsmouth' on fire at Milford Haven in July, 1960.

(Picture: Studio Janwen).

stood by the crippled vessel until the fire was brought under control later that morning.

The fire was fought from the seaward side by the port's fire-fighting tugs, and from the Esso jetty by refinery firemen and the Pembrokeshire Fire Brigade. The fire cost the life of the tanker's chief steward, and three of the crew were seriously hurt. Many of those on board the ship, including two wives, had jumped into the sea and had either swum ashore or were picked up by launches. Another fourteen were taken off the blazing vessel by the tug *Cassiope*, commanded by Derek Saunders.

The *Esso Portsmouth* was towed from the port for repairs, and eventually returned to sea. In 1972, she was sold by Esso and renamed *Winson*, but in January 1975, on a voyage from Galveston to India, she went aground in the South China Sea and was abandoned as a total loss.

An 11,000 ton Liberian registered tanker, the *Dona Marika*, provided the port of Milford Haven with one of its biggest headaches. She had arrived in the Haven from Sicily on August 3rd, 1973, to discharge part of her cargo of high octane spirit, and during

The Angle Life-Boat 'Richard Vernon and Mary Garforth of Leeds' – she went to the aid of the 'Esso Portsmouth' in 1960 and the 'Dona Marika' in 1973, at Milford Haven. (Picture: Haven Photographic).

a storm two days later she was driven aground near Lindsway Bay. The fifty-five year old master of the ship, Captain Markos Palios, radioed that the tanker was in difficulties at about 9 p.m. on Sunday, August 5th. She had begun to drag her anchors in Dale Roads. The force ten gale from the south-south-west had whipped up a rough sea and a heavy swell and the *Dona Marika* was soon aground on rocks, about half-a-

151

mile from the village of St Ishmaels. There was a very real danger of an explosion and most of the five hundred villagers were evacuated from their homes that night.

The Angle Lifeboat had been alerted by St Ann's Head Coastguard soon after the ship went aground and she covered the short distance down the Haven in nineteen minutes. It was now 9.45 p.m. and a number of craft were standing off the tanker, which was rolling heavily with seas breaking over her decks and superstructure. The Coastguard had warned against firing rockets to the tanker, because of her explosive cargo of aviation fuel. Lifeboat Coxswain Rees Holmes decided to run in close to the ship to assess the situation. He afterwards advised the tanker, via the Coastguard, to rig a ladder on the port side amidships and have the crew ready to disembark.

Coxswain Homes managed to put the lifeboat alongside a ladder hanging amidships, but the ship's crew refused to leave the vessel. They wanted the lifeboat to come in on the lee side, but this would have been impossible because of the lack of water. A heavy swell was smashing against the ship's side and when the tanker rolled heavily, water was breaking through the wheelhouse. The lifeboat was rising and falling about 20 feet in the swell, and in the troughs the lifeboat's echo sounder showed less than one foot of water. Indeed, so as not to alarm his own crew, Coxswain Holmes switched off the echo sounder.

The lifeboat made seven consecutive approaches alongside the crippled ship, but on each occasion the tanker's crew refused to leave. Conditions were so bad that the coxswain of a Milford Haven Conservancy Board launch later reported that he thought the lifeboat had foundered. He had lost sight of the lifeboat's masthead blue flashing light, as she rose and fell in the swell, and had feared the worst. As the tanker's crew refused to leave, Coxswain Holmes stood the lifeboat off ready to go in again should an attempt be made to abandon ship from the seaward side. The lifeboat was later requested to set up a breeches buoy, without using a rocket line, but Coxswain Holmes thought that under the circumstances this would have been impracticable.

It was over four hours after high water

The oil tanker 'Dona Marika' on rocks near Lindsway Bay, Milford Haven, in August, 1973. (Picture: Western Telegraph).

when conditions improved sufficiently for a rescue attempt to be made from the shore at 4.15 in the morning. Two members of the Coastguard cliff rescue company made their way to the stern of the tanker, and a Conservancy Board launch and the Angle Lifeboat illuminated the scene with searchlights. The crew began to leave the tanker at 5.15 a.m. and by 6 o'clock the last of the thirty-eight crew members was safely ashore.

The *Dona Marika* now became a salvage problem for the port's Conservancy Board. High octane fuel had escaped from a twenty foot-long gash in her starboard side and anti-pollution craft began cleaning-up operations. During the next three weeks, the ship's remaining cargo of 2,500 tons of spirit and 300 tons of fuel oil was transferred to coastal tankers. Attempts were then made to refloat her, but it was November 13th before she was finally hauled free. The *Dona Marika*'s career was already over. She was sold to Spanish shipbreakers and on December 18th, 1973, she arrived at Alicante after her last voyage.

In March of the following year, the tanker's bell was presented to the village of

Angle Life-Boat Coxswain Rees Holmes with the bronze medal awarded to him for the 'Dona Marika' service in August, 1973. The bronze bar to the medal was presented to him for the rescue of the crew of three of the fishing boat 'Cairnsmore' in December, 1978.

(Picture: Western Telegraph).

154

St Ishmaels in recognition of the efforts of all those involved in the rescue and salvage operations. The gallantry of the Angle Lifeboat Coxswain, Rees Holmes, and his crew resulted in the R.N.L.I. voting Coxswain Holmes the Institution's bronze medal and second coxswain G. Edwards, assistant motor mechanic M. Eynon, and lifeboatmen T. Stewart, R. Callaghan and W. Watkins, received medal service certificates.

It was five years before another oil tanker made as big an impact on Pembrokeshire — but the aftermath of the incident was much worse.

'Christos Bitas grounding 4.5 miles east of the Smalls Light, damage to bottom, leaking oil at sea . . .'

It was shortly after 4.30 on an October afternoon in 1978 that this dramatic message was received by Ilfracombe Radio. The 58,000 ton ship, sailing under the Liberian flag, was on passage from Rotterdam to Belfast on Thursday, October 12th, when she hit the notorious Hats and Barrels reef. She refloated but then headed across the Irish Sea trailing an oil slick 8 miles long and 200 yards wide from damaged tanks. The St

David's Lifeboat was launched and later recalled and the Royal Navy survey ship *H.M.S. Hecate* and two other vessels were standing by the tanker. An R.A.F. helicopter from Brawdy kept the *Christos Bitas* under observation.

By seven that night, the tanker was seven miles away from the Smalls and had altered course, bound at ten knots for her original destination, Belfast. A message from the ship stated that the leakage of oil had ceased, but she was subsequently ordered to stop to reduce the area of pollution risk. She was then $26\frac{1}{2}$ miles off the Irish coast.

Early the next morning, the tanker reported that she was listing to starboard and required immediate assistance. The Rosslare Lifeboat was launched to her aid and took off nineteen people, who were tansferred to the inshore survey ship *H.M.S. Woodlark*. The remaining members of the tanker's crew stayed on board, but the lifeboat stood by in case she was needed. The ship was now listing heavily, with her starboard amidships and forward sections awash. It appeared that the tanker was sinking at the bows. She was then 18 miles from Ireland and a representative of British Petroleum, which had chartered the ship, was airlifted to the vessel. He found the tanker had a 14 degree list, which was not increasing. The ship's owners subsequently accepted help from United Towing and that afternoon, October 13th, the tug *Guardsman* connected a line to the *Christos Bitas*.

The battle was now on to save the ship and to dissipate the 2,000 tons of crude oil which had spilled into the sea. The operation became a race against time as force eight gales were forecast for the area. But by 11 p.m. on October 16th, 10,300 tons of oil had been pumped from the ship into two other tankers. The original oil slick was dangerously close to Pembrokeshire's coastline and the fight to disperse it with detergent was in full swing.

Back on the tanker, pumping operations had been halted on the 17th, but by the end of that week, the ship's cargo had all been transferred. There was a blacker picture on the beaches of Pembrokeshire. Dead sea birds were being washed ashore with every tide and surviving birds were so badly oiled that many would die later in agony. Sixteen grey seal pups were reported to have suffocated when oil reached an island breeding beach.

When the battle to save the *Christos Bitas* was finally won, her owners decided she was not worth repairing and should be sunk. United Towing now made plans to tow the crippled ship out into the Atlantic, where she would be scuttled. On Thursday, October 26th, the remaining crew members of the tanker, and personnel not involved in sinking the casualty, were taken off and two tugs began towing her to a watery grave. Beacuse of worsening weather conditions, the *Christos Bitas* did not reach the agreed scuttling point 580 miles west of Ireland. Severe gales were forecast and it was decided to sink her 280 miles nearer to Ireland in an area approved for wreck disposal. At 2.40 p.m. on Tuesday, October 31st, the tanker was scuttled in 2,600 fathoms of water. Her story was at an end, but she left behind a deadly legacy of pollution on beaches along the Welsh, West Country and Irish coastlines.

During the whole of the *Christos Bitas*

The battle to save the stricken oil tanker 'Christos Bitas' in October, 1978, involved transferring her cargo of crude oil to other tankers. Here – part of her deck awash – she wallows alongside the tanker 'Esso York'. (Picture: Western Telegraph).

affair, a total of sixty-six vessels were used, forty-eight of which were engaged in anti-pollution measures. Reconnaissance and spraying aircraft also took part and helicopters from R.A.F. Brawdy and the Royal Naval Air Station at Culdrose flew over fifty sorties.

It is estimated that nine-thousand birds including eleven different species died as a result of *Christos Bitas* pollution. Had the disaster occurred in the birds' breeding season the death toll would have been even higher.

Bibliography

Body, Geoffrey. *British Paddle Steamers* (David & Charles, 1971)
  British Channel Pilot, 1859 (Bradford Barton reprint, 1978)
  British Vessels Lost at Sea, 1914-18 (Patrick Stephens, 1977)
  British Vessels Lost at Sea, 1939-45 (Patrick Stephens, 1976)
Colledge, J.J. *Ships of the Royal Navy Vol. II* (David & Charles, 1970)
Dittmar, F.J. & Colledge, J.J. *British Warships, 1914-1919* (Ian Allen, 1972)
Edwards, J. Dudley. *St Ishmaels – The Story and History of a Village* (1972)
Edwards, J. Dudley & Thorne, Roland G. *A Supplement to St Ishmaels*
Evans, Lieutenant-Commander Charles E. *Memoirs* (Western Mail, 1946)
Farr, A.D. *Let Not the Deep* (Impulse, 1973)
Farr, Grahame. *Chepstow Ships* (Chepstow Society, 1954)
Farr, Grahame. *West Country Passenger Steamers* (Stephenson & Sons, 1956)
Farr, Grahame. *Wreck and Rescue in the Bristol Channel II. The Story of the Welsh Lifeboats* (Bradford Barton, 1967)
Fenton, R. *A Historical Tour Through Pembrokeshire* (1811)
Freeman, Eric. *The Solva Saga* (1958)
Gardner, Don. *Vagabond Book of St David's/Fishguard* (Gomer)
Gray, Edwyn A. *The Killing Time* (Pan, 1975)
Greenhill, Basil. *The Merchant Schooners. Vols I & II* (David & Charles, 1968)
Gwynedd Archive Service. *Maritime Wales No. 2* (1977)
Hague, Douglas B. & Christie, Rosemary. *Lighthouses: Their Architecture, History and Archaeology* (Gomer, 1975)
Hampson, Desmond G. & Middleton, George W. *The Story of the St David's Lifeboats* (1974)
Hocking, Charles. *Dictionary of Disasters at Sea in the Age of Steam, 1824-1962. Vols I & II* (Lloyds Register of Shipping, 1969)
Hoehling, A.A. *The Great War at Sea* (Arthur Barker, 1965)

Howells, Roscoe. *Cliffs of Freedom* (H. G. Walters, 1961)

Howells, Roscoe. *The Sounds Between* (H. G. Walters, 1968)

Jackson, Derrick. *Lighthouses of England and Wales* (David & Charles, 1975)

James, Rev. H. Whitby. *Castlemartin* (1946)

Jones, Susan Campbell. *Welsh Sail* (Gomer, 1976)

Jones, Commander E. H. Stuart. *The Last Invasion of Britain* (University of Wales, 1950)

Kahre, George. *The Last Tall Ships* (Conway Maritime, 1978)

Langmaid, Captain Kenneth. *The Sea, Thine Enemy* (Jarrolds, 1966)

Leach, A. L. *A Tenby Artist: Charles Norris (1779-1858),* (Tenby Observer and County News, 1949)

Lenton, H.T. *German Warships of the Second World War* (Macdonald & Jane's, 1975)

Lockley, R.M. *Dream Island Days* (H. F. & G. Witherby, 1943)

Lund, Paul and Ludlam, Harry. *The War of the Landing Craft* (Foulsham, 1976)

March, Edgar J. *Sailing Trawlers* (David & Charles, 1970)

McNeill, D.B. *Irish Passenger Steamship Services. Vol. II: The South of Ireland* (David & Charles, 1969)

Morgan, Mary. *A Tour of Milford Haven* (John Stockdale, 1795)

North, A.J.D. *Royal Navy Coastal Forces* (Almark, 1972)

Osborne, Wendy. *Princes, Pigs and People of Tenby* (Five Arches Press, 1974)

R.N.L.I. *Lifeboat Wales '77*

R.N.L.I. *Stories of the Lifeboats* (1956)

Sawyer, L.A. & Mitchell, W.H. *The Liberty Ships* (David & Charles, 1970)

Slade, W. J. and Greenhill, Basil. *Westcountry Coasting Ketches* (Conway Maritime, 1974)

Stickings, Thomas G. *The Story of Saundersfoot* (H. G. Walters, 1970)

Timmins, H. Thornhill. *Nooks and Corners of Pembrokeshire* (Elliot Stock, 1895)

Vince, Charles. *Storm on the Waters* (Hodder & Stoughton, 1946)

Wales Tourist Board. *A Glimpse of the Past* (1978)

Warburton, F.W. *The History of Solva* (Blackheath, 1944)

Warner, Oliver. *The Lifeboat Service* (Cassell, 1974)

Whymper, F. *The Sea* (Cassell, Petter and Galpin, 1878)

Zanelli, Leo. *Shipwrecks Around Britain* (Kaye & Ward, 1970)

Zanelli, Leo. *Unknown Shipwrecks Around Britain* (Kaye & Ward, 1974)

Records, manuscripts etc.

Public Record Office (Kew): ADM 1/5386. Admiralty court martials March-April, 1808. H.M.S. Leda.
Public Record Office (Chancery Lane): SP.29/250. No.186. Loss of the Amity.
Pembrokeshire Record Office (Dyfed Archives): HPR 84/34. Notebook of James Nash, Solva. DX/96/4. The Ballad of Bitches Rock.
Royal National Lifeboat Institution: Various records relating to Pembrokeshire lifeboats.

Newspapers, Journals etc.

Haverfordwest and Milford Haven Telegraph
Lifeboat Journal (R.N.L.I.)
Lloyds List
Marine News (World Ship Society)
Pembroke County Guardian
Pembrokeshire Herald and General Advertiser
Sea Breezes
South Wales Evening Post
Tenby Observer
Western Mail
Western Telegraph
West Wales Guardian

Chronology of Wreck and Rescue

Date	Ship	Location
1668, December 16th	*Amity*	Ramsey Sound
1740s	*Mayflower*	Off Skomer Island
1773, January 8th	*Phoebe and Peggy*	Off Solva
1780s	Unknown	Bishops and Clerks
1791, January 4th	*Increase*	Druidston Haven
1797	Lord Cawdor's yacht	Off Linney Head
1808, January 31st	*H.M.S. Leda*	West Angle Bay
1810, December 25th	*Linen Hall*	Druidston Haven
1812, December 30th	*Fortitude*	Smalls
1815, December 19th	*Warren*	Ramsey Sound
1825, October	*Horatio*	Fishguard Bay
1829	*Dorchester*	Beached Tenby
1833, February 19th	*Felicita*	Sandy Haven Bay
1833, February 21st	*Frederick*	St David's Head
1835	*Hunter*	Tenby
1835, September	*Neptune*	St Govan's Head
1836, February 17th	*Trevor*	Fishguard Bay
1836, October	*Wheatsheaf*	Saundersfoot
1837, April 19th	*Albion*	Near Marloes
1839, February 8th	*Edinburgh*	Linney Head
1839, February 23rd	*Durham*	Saundersfoot
1843, September 1st	*Queen*	Skokholm Island
1844, August 4th	*Richard*	Tenby
1846, November 20th	*Victoria*	Off Solva

1848, December 6th	*Dispatch*	Linney Head
1849, January	*Lady Kenmare*	Goodwick Sands
1850, June 4th	*John Guise*	St David's Head
1850, November 19th	*Maria*	Pill Point, Milford Haven
1852, January 14th	*George and Francis*	West Angle Bay
1855, February 25th	*Morna*	North Bishop
1855, December 18th	*Agenoria*	Tenby
1855, December 18th	*Alexandra*	Tenby
1856, February 6th	*Great Duke*	Near Bullslaughter Bay
1857, April 23rd	*Robert and Mary*	Linney Head
1859, October 26th	*Wave*	Freshwater West
1859, November 6th	*Policy*	Monkstone Point
1860, February 28th	*Nimrod*	St David's Head
1860, March 16th	*Request*	St Bride's Bay
1860, April 5th	*Surprise*	St Bride's Bay
1861, February 19th	*Harmony*	Freshwater West
1862	Unknown	Freshwater West
1862, April 1st	*Mars*	Linney Head
1862, October 17th	*Oak*	Off Solva
1863, March 17th	*Francis*	Newport
1866, November 10th	*Alfred Eliza*	Mill Bay
1866, November 10th	*Commodore*	Mill Bay
1866, November 10th	*Eliza and Jane*	Mill Bay
1866, November 10th	*Hope*	Mill Bay
1866, November 10th	*Isobel*	Mill Bay
1866, November 10th	*King of the Forest*	Mill Bay
1868, August 22nd	*Emily Ann*	Caldey Roads
1868, August 22nd	*Nameless*	Caldey Roads
1870, October 12th	*Transit*	Ramsey Sound

1870, November 23rd	*Anne Davies*	Ramsey Sound
1870, November 23rd	*Chester*	Ramsey Sound
1870, November 23rd	*Prima*	Ramsey Sound
1872, June 5th	*Mersey*	South Bishop
1872, November 10th	*John and Grace*	Goodwick Sands
1872, November 10th	*Mary*	Goodwick Sands
1873, October 22nd	*Sarah*	St Bride's Bay
1874	*Alaric*	St Bride's Bay
1874, October 28th	*Amelia*	Linney Head
1875, November 14th	*Elinor and Mary*	Goodwick Sands
1875, November 14th	*Independence*	Goodwick Sands
1875, November 14th	*Laura*	Fishguard Bay
1875, November 14th	*Princess Royal*	Goodwick Sands
1875, November 25th	*Breeze*	Off St Ann's Head
1877, February 23rd	*Adventure*	Fishguard Bay
1877, February 23rd	*B. F. Nash*	Fishguard Bay
1877, February 23rd	*George Evans*	Fishguard Bay
1877, February 23rd	*Supply*	Fishguard Bay
1877, November 11th	*Mystic Tie*	Ramsey Island
1881, April 16th	*Amazon Ense*	St David's Head
1881, October 26th	*Lass O'Gowrie*	Marloes Sands
1882	*Guiding Star*	Whitesands Bay
1882, January	*Thomas Vaughan*	Jack Sound
1883, September 26th	*Slaney*	Dale Roads
1884, January 29th	*Rhiwabon*	Smalls
1886, February 28th	*Glenisla*	St David's Head
1887, May 20th	*George Moore*	Smalls
1887, June	*Gulliver*	Smalls
1889, October 8th	*Reliance*	Newport

1890s	*Annie Park*	St Govan's Head
1891, April 30th	*Drumburlie*	Smalls
1892, May 15th	*Earl of Aberdeen*	Hats and Barrels
1892, May 28th	*Koh-i-Noor*	St David's Head
1892, November 25th	*Musgrave*	Pen Clegyr
1893, May 13th	*Rowena*	Smalls
1893, November 18th	*Evviva*	Fishguard Bay
1893, November 18th	*Warrenpoint*	Goodwick Sands
1893, December 8th	*Ellen*	Grassholm Island
1894, January 30th	*Loch Shiel*	Thorn Island
1894, October 30th	*Tormes*	Linney Head
1897, July 25th	*Hibernia*	Smalls
1898, January 21st	*Mareca*	Off St Govan's Head
1898, August	*Baron Ardrossan*	Porthgain
1900s	*Humber*	Brimstone Rocks
1903, January 25th	*Graffoe*	Ramsey Island
1903, December 15th	*Count C'Aspremont*	Ramsey Sound
1904, May	*Edith Crossfield*	North Bishop
1906	*Shamrock*	Pen-y-Holt Stack
1906, November 14th	*Ross*	Bishops and Clerks
1907	*Princess Irene*	Brimstone Rocks
1907, November 3rd	*Netherholme*	Pen-y-Holt Stack
1908, January 11th	*Tantallon Castle*	12 miles off Smalls
1908, September 28th	*Szent Istvan*	Ramsey Island
1909, August 5th	*Langton Grange*	North Bishop
1910, October 12th	*Democrat*	Ramsey Sound
1910, October 12th	*Gem* (Lifeboat)	Ramsey Sound
1911, January 12th	*Agnes Craig*	Fishguard Bay
1911, January 12th	*Democrat*	Fishguard Bay

1911, January 12th	*Dynamo*	Fishguard Bay
1911, January 12th	*Fishguard*	Fishguard Bay
1911, January 12th	*Lizzie Edith*	Fishguard Bay
1911, October 7th	*Sarah Macdonald*	Smalls
1913, May 24th	*Cambro*	Smalls
1914, August 15th	*Ellerbeck*	Hats and Barrels
1914, August 22nd	*Alpha*	Off St David's Head
1914, September 6th	*Endcliffe*	Beached Porthmelgan
1915, March 27th	*Aguila*	47 miles S.W. of Smalls
1915, March 28th	*Falaba*	38 miles W. of Smalls
1915, June 8th	*Express*	44 miles S.S.W. of Smalls
1915, June 8th	*Susannah*	40 miles S.S.W. of Smalls
1915, June 12th	*Bellglade*	70 miles W.S.W. of St Ann's Head
1915, June 12th	*Crown of India*	70 miles W.S.W. of St Ann's Head
1915, June 15th	*Strathnairn*	25 miles N. by E. of Bishops and Clerks
1915, June 27th	*Indrani*	40 miles W. of Smalls
1915, June 28th	*Dumfriesshire*	25 miles S.W. of Smalls
1915, July 9th	*Ellesmere*	48 miles S.W. of Smalls
1915, July 9th	*Ito*	48 miles S.W. of Smalls
1915, August 17th	*Glenby*	30 miles N. of Smalls
1915, August 17th	*The Queen*	40 miles N.N.E. of Smalls
1915, August 17th	*Thornfield*	25 miles N.N.E. of Smalls
1915, November 13th	*Calburga*	Pen Brush, Strumble Head
1915, November 13th	*Cautiose*	Goodwick Sands
1915, November 13th	*Dinorwic*	Goodwick Sands
1915, November 13th	*Echo*	Goodwick Sands
1915, November 13th	*Emlyn*	Fishguard Harbour
1915, November 13th	*Flora*	Fishguard Harbour
1915, November 13th	*Formosa*	North Bishop

1915, December 14th	*Susanna*	Off St Ann's Head
1915, December 25th	*Van Stirum*	8 miles S.S.W. of Smalls
1915, December 27th	*Ferndale*	St Ann's Head
1915, December 27th	*Ladysmith*	Off St Ann's Head
1915, December 31st	*Satrap*	Near Manorbier
1916, April 3rd	*Pecheur*	Off Smalls
1916, September 2nd	*Kelvinia*	9 miles S. by W. of Caldey Island
1916, September 26th	*Loch Shiel*	Off St Ann's Head
1916, December 26th	*Agnes*	15 miles S.W. by W. of St Ann's Head
1917, February 11th	*Lycia*	25 miles N.E. by N. of South Bishop
1917, February 11th	*Olivia*	25 miles N. of South Bishop
1917, February 11th	*Voltaire*	25 miles N.E. by N. of South Bishop
1917, February 12th	*Pinna*	Beached Milford Haven
1917, February 13th	*Friendship*	Off Smalls
1917, February 13th	*Zircon*	26 miles S.W. of Smalls
1917, February 14th	*Inishowen Head*	Off Skokholm Island
1917, February 15th	*Afton*	23 miles N. by E. of Strumble Head
1917, February 20th	*Leysian*	7 miles off Strumble Head
1917, February 24th	*Cymric Prince*	North Bishop
1917, February 26th	*Hannah Croasdell*	4 miles W. $^3/_4$ N. of St Ann's Head
1917, March 1st	*Drina*	Off Skokholm Island
1917, March 9th	*Inverlogie*	15 miles S.W. of Smalls
1917, March 25th	*Evangel*	Off St Ann's Head
1917, April	*Borrowdale*	Off South Pembrokeshire
1917, April 17th	*Dantzic*	30 miles S. by W. of St Ann's Head
1917, April 17th	*William Shepherd*	30 miles S. by W. of St Ann's Head
1917, May 4th	*Strumble*	10 miles N.N.E. of Strumble Head
1917, May 4th	*Victorious*	10 miles N.N.E. of Strumble Head
1917, May 21st	*Colonian*	North Bishop

1917, May 29th	*Bestwood*	12 miles S.W. of South Bishop
1917, August 11th	*Gloriosa*	12 miles S. by W. of Caldey Island
1917, August 12th	*Eleazar*	25 miles S.W. by W. of St Ann's Head
1917, September 15th	*Saint Jacques*	Off St Ann's Head
1917, October 3rd	*Hurst*	Off Skokholm Island
1917, October 15th	*Active III*	Off St Ann's Head
1917, October 20th	*Ionian*	Off St Govan's Head
1917, November 18th	*Gisella*	Off Skokholm Island
1917, December 12th	*Charleston*	30 miles W. of Smalls
1917, December 22nd	*Colemere*	35 miles W. of Smalls
1917, December 28th	*Lord Derby*	7 miles S.W. by S. of St Ann's Head
1918, January 2nd	*Boston City*	11 miles W. $\frac{1}{2}$ N. of St Ann's Head
1918, January 3rd	*John*	Off Smalls
1918, February 24th	*Renfrew*	8 miles S.W. of St Ann's Head
1918, March 23rd	*Jane Gray*	14 miles N. by W. of Smalls
1918, March 24th	*John G. Walter*	20 miles S.W. of Smalls
1918, April 7th	*Boscastle*	14 miles N.N.W. of Strumble Head
1918, April 12th	*Wilson*	10 miles N.W. of Smalls
1918, April 16th	*Select*	Off St Govan's Head
1918, April 21st	*Landonia*	27 miles N. by W. $\frac{1}{2}$ W. of Strumble Head
1918, April 26th	*Ethel*	19 miles N. $\frac{3}{4}$ E. of Smalls
1918, April 26th	*Gresham*	18 miles N.W. by N. of Strumble Head
1918, May 9th	*Baron Ailsa*	18 miles W.N.W. of Smalls
1918, May 9th	*Wileysike*	8 miles S.W. of St Ann's Head
1918, June 9th	*Vandalia*	18 miles W.N.W. of Smalls
1918, July 3rd	*Florrie*	Off Linney Head
1918, August 24th	*Virent*	38 miles W. by S. of Smalls
1918, August 27th	*Ant Cassar*	30 miles N.N.W. of Strumble Head

1918, September 16th	*Serula*	13½ miles N.E. ½ N. of Strumble Head
1918, September 26th	*Tampa*	Bristol Channel
1918, October 4th	*Hirano Maru*	Irish Sea
1918, October 16th	*Pentwyn*	20 miles N.E. by N. of Smalls
1918, October 20th	*Emily Millington*	13 miles N.N.E. of South Bishop
1920, December 3rd	*Hermina*	Fishguard Bay
1921, September	*Meridian*	Smalls
1922, April 16th	*Lusitania I*	Off Cemaes Head
1923, January 31st	*Mar del Plata*	Hats and Barrels
1923, February 26th	*Tevija*	Off Tenby
1927, April 18th	*Wrestler*	Freshwater West
1927, December 9th	*Portland*	St Bride's Bay
1928, February 24th	*Alice Williams*	Skokholm Island
1929, November 25th	*Molesey*	Midland Island, Skomer
1936, January 5th	*Shore Breeze*	St Ann's Head
1936, January 6th	*Ethel May*	Dale Roads
1936, February	*Nellie Fleming*	Off South Pembrokeshire
1938, January 15th	*Fermanagh*	Off Woolhouse Rocks
1938, October 23rd	*Lonsdale*	Midland Island, Skomer
1939, November 1st	*Mervyn*	10 miles S.E. of Smalls
1940, January 27th	*Adamantios J. Pithis*	St Ann's Head
1940, February 3rd	*Belpariel*	Caldey Island
1940, February 26th	*Ida*	Off St David's Head
1940, August 18th	*Valeria*	Off Smalls
1940, August 22nd	*Thorold*	Off Smalls
1940, October 9th	*Alderney Queen*	Off Grassholm Island
1940, November 11th	*Ardmore*	Irish Sea
1940, November 21st	*Dakotian*	Dale Roads

1940, November 22nd	*Pikepool*	Off Linney Head
1940, November 24th	*Behar*	Beached Milford Haven
1940, November 24th	*Preserver*	Milford Haven
1941, January 27th	*Beemsterdyk*	12 miles off Smalls
1941, February 3rd	*M.G.B. 12*	Milford Haven
1941, March 3rd	*Port Townsville*	Off St David's Head
1941, March 12th	*Empire Frost*	8 miles off Smalls
1941, March 21st	*London II*	18 miles S.S.E. of Caldey Island
1941, March 21st	*Millisle*	12 miles off Caldey Island
1941, March 22nd	*St Fintan*	7 miles N.W. of Smalls
1941, March 27th	*Faraday*	Off St Ann's Head
1941, March 27th	*Meg Merrilies*	Off St Govan's Lightvessel
1941, April 1st	*Hidlefjord*	Off Smalls
1941, April 1st	*San Conrado*	Off Smalls
1941, April 28th	*Johanna Caroline*	Milford Haven
1941, May 9th	*Tankerton Towers*	Off St Govan's Lightvessel
1941, May 18th	*Begerin*	Off South Bishop
1941, June 7th	*Examination Vessel No. 10*	Off St Ann's Head
1941, June 11th	*Baron Carnegie*	Off Strumble Head
1941, June 13th	*St Patrick*	12 miles off Strumble Head
1941, July 5th	*Fowey Rose*	20 miles S.W. of St Govan's Head
1941, July 6th	*Westfield*	Off St Govan's Head
1941, September 7th	*Empire Gunner*	12 miles N.W. of Strumble Head
1941, September 15th	*Daru*	15 miles N.W. of Smalls
1942, January 27th	*Eveline*	Off St Ann's Head
1942, April 5th	*Empire Beacon*	Off St Ann's Head
1943, January 1st	*Empire Panther*	8 miles off Strumble Head
1943, March 13th	*Moray*	Off St Ann's Head
1943, April 25th	*LCG 15*	Off St Ann's Head

1943, April 26th	*LCG 16*	Off St Ann's Head
1943, August 20th	*Athelduchess*	Off Smalls
1943, December 18th	*Thor*	Off St Ann's Head
1944, December 3rd	*Collier PLM 21*	Off St Ann's Head
1944, December 10th	*Dan Beard*	7 miles W. of Strumble Head
1945, January 9th	*Jonas Lie*	Off Grassholm Island
1945, February 28th	*Norfolk Coast*	7 miles off South Bishop
1945, March 2nd	*King Edgar*	20 miles N.W. of St David's Head
1945, March 7th	*U-1302*	25 miles N.W. of St David's Head
1945, March 28th	*Antonio*	Off St Ann's Head
1945, July 16th	*Walter L. M. Russ*	Grassholm Island
1945, October 7th	*Juta*	Off Caldey Island
1946, March 27th	*Nicolaou Virginia*	Flimstone Head
1949, October 21st	*Cydonia*	Beached Angle Bay
1952, August 17th	*Enchantress*	Near St Govan's Head
1953, September 21st	*St Govan's Lightvessel*	Off St Govan's Head
1954, July 28th	*Progress*	Beached Angle Bay
1954, November 27th	*Gramsbergen*	Fishguard Bay
1954, November 27th	*World Concord*	Off North Pembrokeshire
1954, November 30th	*Ability*	Scotch Bay, Milford Haven
1956, November 8th	*Notre Dame de Fatima*	Off Skokholm Island
1960, July 9th	*Esso Portsmouth*	Milford Haven
1961, June 25th	*Etrog*	Beached Dale
1961, September 10th	*Iliad*	Monkstone Point
1961, December 10th	*Wiema*	St Bride's Bay
1964, March 20th	*Barking*	Mill Bay
1967, February 14th	*Lucy*	Jack Sound
1967, March 1st	*Luminence*	Smalls
1968, April 15th	*William Rhodes Moorhouse*	Fishguard Bay

1969, December 14th	*Metric*	Off Strumble Head
1972, December 18th	*Dolwen*	Off Strumble Head
1973, August 5th	*Dona Marika*	Milford Haven
1974, December 19th	*Attacker*	Newgale
1977, March 27th	*El Tambo*	Fishguard Bay
1978, October 12th	*Christos Bitas*	Hats and Barrels
1979, January 26th	*Balholm*	Off Linney Head

Index

178

Royal Aircraft Establishment, Aberporth, 52, 75
Royal Canadian Navy, 126
Royal Marines, 91, 94
Royal Maritime Auxiliary Service vessels, 52, 55
Royal Navy, 13, 14, 21, 46, 55, 112, 117, 123, 125, 129, 155, 158; air station, Brawdy, 21, 81, 148; air station, Culdrose, 158; base, Milford Haven, 102, 111, 122, 126; Flag Officer, Milford Haven, 125, 126; helicopters, 21, 81, 148
Royal Air Force, 120; Brawdy, 21, 57, 155, 158; helicopters, 18, 21, 57, 155, 158
Runcorn, 82
Russia, 102, 143
Rye, 90
Rye, H.M.S., 14

S
Saddle Point, 45
'Sailo'r Rest and Bethel', Milford Haven, 100
St Ann's Head, 15, 18, 34, 36, 61, 91, 102, 104, 107, 109, 110, 113, 114, 118, 121, 123, 124, 127-129, 152; Coastguard, 18, 102, 152; lighthouse, 15, 87, 89
St Bride's, 73
St Bride's Bay, 38, 66, 72-75, 77
St Catherine's Island, 39; Fort, 39
St David's, 27, 34, 38, 39, 67, 89, 97, 98, 114, 146; Head, 34, 42, 46, 48, 65, 85, 86, 88, 99, 103, 117, 126; Peninsula, 69

St David's lifeboat station, 20, 38, 46, 93, 97, 112, 121, 122, 148; lifeboats, 20, 27, 31, 32, 34, 36, 38, 46, 55, 68-73, 82, 91, 93, 95, 97, 98, 112, 113, 117, 119, 121, 122, 125, 146, 148, 155; hon. secretaries, Captain John Rees, 70; Dr Joseph Soar, 38, 39, 93, 112, 146; coxswains, Ivor Arnold, 36, 38, 39, 70, 97; David Hicks, 46, 70; Dai Lewis, 34; Sydney Mortimer, 29-33; William Narbett, 68, 69; John Stephens, 27, 31, 72; William Watts Williams, 91, 93, 95, 146, 148, 149; second coxswain, Dai Lewis, 149; motor mechanic, George Jordan, 149; assistant motor mechanic, Gwilym Davies, 149; bowman, William Rowlands (acting), 149; lifeboatmen, Ieuan Bateman, 34, Richard Chisholm, 149, G. Davies, 112, J. Jenkins, 125, D. Lewis, 112, William Morris, 149, James Price, 27, 31, Howell Roberts, 149, Henry Rowlands, 27, 31
St Elvis, 66
St Fintan, 117
St George's Channel, 94
St Govan's Chapel, 67
St Govan's Head, 16, 85, 109, 110, 120, 138, 141, 144
St Gowan (lightvessel), 16, 118, 139
St Ishmael's, 73, 152, 155
Saint Jacques (steamship), 108
St Justinian's, 27, 31; Chapel, 67